EMILY DICKINSON IN EUROPE

Her Literary Reputation in Selected Countries

Ann Lilliedahl

UNIVERSITY
PRESS OF
AMERICA

Copyright © 1981 by

University Press of America, Inc.

P.O. Box 19101, Washington, D.C. 20036

Library of Congress Cataloging in Publication Data

Lilliedahl, Ann.
    Emily Dickinson in Europe.

    Bibliography: p.
    Includes index.
    1. Dickinson, Emily, 1830-1886--Criticism and
interpretation. 2. Dickinson, Emily, 1830-1886--
Appreciation--Europe. 3. Books and reading--
Europe. 4. Europe--Intellectual life--20th century.
I. Title.
PS1541.Z5L45   811'.4   81-40308
ISBN 0-8191-1890-7
ISBN 0-8191-1891-5 (pbk.)   AACR2

198014

Library of Congress Catalog Card Number: **81-40308**

To my Mother and Father

ACKNOWLEDGMENTS

Without the knowledgable and devoted work of my mother, this book might neither have been indexed nor, indeed, as extensively proofread. Our proofreading was shared by Mrs. Helen Viereck, who unselfishly devoted many a day to such an uninspiring task.

I am indebted to Professor Lars von Haartman for the frontispiece, one of his many translations and illustrations of Emily Dickinson poems. Also, I am grateful for the permission to use his personal viewpoints of the poetry of Emily Dickinson and others as reflected in an extensive correspondence with me. Finally, Professor Thomas W. Ford gave me his permission to use an original idea of his which came up during a conversation between us regarding a Dickinson poem.

vi

Table of Contents

479

En dårskap medan vårn är ung
är hälsan också för en kung.
Men, Herre, se till klownens själ
som ser på allting stort som hänt,
ditt grönskande experiment,
som sin privata ägodel.

Emily Dickinson's poem
"A little Madness in the Spring"
translated into Swedish and
illustrated by Lars von Haartman

ix

I. Introduction

Emily Dickinson is a poet who wrote at a time when, according to F. O. Matthiessen in his *American Renaissance*, American letters had reached a maturity worthy of comparison to European literature.[1] She is also a poet whose main concerns, such as nature, death, and love, are universal and therefore of interest to any nation. The European interest in Emily Dickinson can best be understood by a survey and review of foreign criticism of the poet. The purpose of this study is to make such a survey available in English translation.

Edgar Allan Poe, Henry James, and Ernest Hemingway are among those major American writers whose foreign reputations have so far attracted the attention of American scholars. For obvious reasons, namely the close psychological and intellectual ties with France of the first two writers, those studies focused on the French reception.[2] Similarly, a study has been made of the reception of Hemingway in Germany[3] and one of Poe in Scan-

[1]F. O. Matthiessen, *American Renaissance* (London and New York: Oxford University Press, 1941).

[2]The most comprehensive study of the relationship between Poe and France is Patrick F. Quinn, *The French Face of Edgar Poe* (Carbondale: Southern Illinois University Press, 1971). This study includes criticism of Poe by Baudelaire, Mallarmé, and Valéry, in addition to American viewpoints. For information regarding the relationship between James and France, see in particular Oscar Cargill, *The Novels of Henry James* (New York: Macmillan, 1961), and Leon Edel, *Henry James: The Middle Years* (Philadelphia: Lippincott, 1962).

[3]Wayne E. Kvam, *Hemingway in Germany: The Fiction, the Legend, and the Critics* (Athens: Ohio University Press, 1973).

dinavia.[4] The last two studies concentrate on one
small, clearly defined, cultural area--presumably
because the authors are knowledgeable in German
and Swedish: Carl L. Anderson (of the Poe study)
is, in fact, of Swedish ancestry.[5]

One of the few critics to deal with a full
picture of European criticism of a single author
is Roger Asselineau in his The Literary Reputation
of Hemingway in Europe.[6] His function, however,
was primarily that of editor. His method was to
assign the responsibility for a given national
critical picture to the "best man" in that country.
So, for instance, Lars Åhnebrink was responsible
for Sweden, Sigmund Skard for Norway, and Heinrich
Straumann, of the University of Zürich, Switzerland, for the introduction. Asselineau deals ex-
pertly with the French response. The book, of
course, is of interest as a first-rate collection
of essays. A drawback, perhaps, is the lack of a
co-ordinating evaluator capable of dealing with
all the material in its original language. Thus,
there is no "conclusion" and no attempt has been
made to relate the different contributions to each
other.

In this study, I deal with Emily Dickinson's
different receptions in Sweden, Norway, Denmark,

[4]Carl L. Anderson, Poe in Northlight: The
Scandinavian Response to His Life and Work (Dur-
ham: Duke University Press, 1973).

[5]Another study by the same scholar is Carl L.
Anderson, The Swedish Acceptance of American
Literature (Philadelphia: University of Pennsylvania Press, 1957). Anderson's work spans the
late nineteenth century through the 1930's, mainly treating prose writers such as Jack London,
Theodore Dreiser, and Sinclair Lewis.

[6]Roger Asselineau, ed., The Literary Reputation of Hemingway in Europe (New York: New York
University Press, 1965).

France, and Germany. Also surveyed were the two other German-speaking countries, Austria and German-speaking Switzerland, and the former Danish colony of Iceland. In Austria, with the exception of the one dissertation mentioned in chapter V, no dissertations or theses seem to have been written on Emily Dickinson between 1886 -1977, the years surveyed. In addition, I have found no books, chapters, or articles on the poet. In Switzerland, the situation is somewhat different. Some few critics have written on Dickinson in German-speaking Switzerland, but because the material is very limited and the critics not major, those items have been incorporated into the German material. Roland Hagenbüchle, however, is an exception in the sense that he is a major critic, but since he has relocated from Zürich, Switzerland, to Wuppertal, Germany, he, too, appears in the chapter on Germany proper. In the cases where the author of an item is Swiss, this has been indicated either in the text or in the footnote. Although Iceland might conceivably have produced some scholarship on Dickinson in Danish, that is not the case. While I do not claim that either the French or the German material is complete, I believe that few works of great significance have been omitted. The material from these countries is substantial enough to give a significant and reliable picture of Emily Dickinson in the eyes of the critics and translators concerned. The situation regarding the Scandinavian countries and Swedish-speaking Finland is somewhat different. I have managed to secure material to an extent that would seem to represent a fairly complete picture of the reception of Emily Dickinson in those countries. This study covers the time beginning with the death of Emily Dickinson in 1886 ending with and including the year 1977. The English titles given for translated Dickinson poems and the numbers sometimes used by me are from the Johnson 1955 edition.[7]

[7]Thomas H. Johnson, ed., The Poems of Emily Dickinson. 3 vols. (Cambridge, Mass.: Harvard University Press, 1955).

My chapter divisions are by country, or, in the case of Norway and Denmark, by cultural grouping of countries. Each chapter is set up in the same way, i.e., chronologically. In the concluding chapter, I have related the receptions within the different countries to each other. National preferences, biases, cultural characteristics, as well as political-historical backgrounds, constitute a frame of reference for this chapter.

In my translations and summaries, I have aimed for accuracy, directness, and simplicity, hoping by these means to convey the intent of the original material without distortion. My policy has been, in the main, to avoid value judgments of the criticism, for it is not the purpose of this study to engage in criticism of criticism. My primary purpose has been to make available to the English reader an objective presentation of European criticism of Emily Dickinson.

II. Sweden and Swedish-speaking Finland

The poetry of Emily Dickinson came late to
Sweden in the sense of being generally accepted.
In the 1920's, when the poet was receiving recog-
nition in her homeland, the best known general
reference book in Sweden, Nordisk Familjebok [The
Nordic Family Book], had no entry concerning her.

The reasons for this late interest are many.
In the 1920's, the Swedes already had a relatively large number of highly sophisticated poetic
innovators, such as Gustaf Fröding, Erik Axel
Karlfeldt, Dan Andersson, and Birger Sjöberg.
Karlfeldt was awarded the Nobel Prize posthumously
and was himself a member of The Eighteen[1] and Permanent Secretary of the Swedish Academy until his
death in 1931. In the sense of using everyday
imagery to shock the reader into recognition,
Fröding and Karlfeldt were well established
pioneers already in the beginning of the twentieth
century, with Andersson and Sjöberg as two of the
many followers. Sjöberg, in particular, preferred
images such as a maid dusting dead flies from the
furniture to convey more profound observations;
such devices are commonly found in Emily Dickinson's poetry. In a country where daring poetry,
together perhaps with drama, has always held a
strong position, Emily Dickinson was neither
strikingly "ungrammatical" nor an otherwise
unorthodox poet. Lars von Haartman, whose congenial and skillful translations of Emily Dickinson will be discussed later, finds no direct influence of Emily Dickinson on Swedish poets. The

[1]"The Eighteen" is synonymous with the
Swedish Academy, the famous Swedish society that
awards the annual Nobel Prizes. It was founded in
1786 by King Gustav III after the pattern of
l'Académie française. The most prestigious position in the Academy is that of Permanent Secretary.

reason, according to Haartman, is that "she
arrived too late" on the Swedish poetic scene,
which was already well into experiments with "half-
rhyme" and varied metrical patterns.²

Other reasons for the late interest in Emily
Dickinson were partly political. Lars Åhnebrink,
in The Literary Reputation of Hemingway in Europe,
attempts to explain the difficulties that American
writers encountered in Sweden from the end of the
nineteenth century up to perhaps 1930 when Sinclair
Lewis was awarded the Nobel Prize. The Swedes,
Åhnebrink argues, had originally shared the
European idealistic attitudes toward colonial
America in the hope that America would fulfill the
aspirations of European immigrants. At the turn
of the century, a certain distaste for American
culture developed, as can be seen generally in
essays and comments on America by three Swedish
critics, Per Hallström, Henning Berger, and Gustaf
Hellström. The first two critics were also members of the Swedish Academy. They followed Knut
Hamsun, the famous Norwegian novelist and critic,
whose direct attacks on America had a lasting
effect. This hostile attitude eventually weaken-
ed during the twenties, and after Lewis' Nobel
Prize in 1930, American literature gained some
acceptance. In 1919 Anders Österling, poet and
Permanent Secretary of the Swedish Academy, emphasized the new interest in the "transatlantic
uniqueness" of American literature.³

²Letter received from Lars von Haartman, 7
September 1977.

³Lars Åhnebrink, "Hemingway in Sweden," The
Literary Reputation of Hemingway in Europe, ed.
Roger Asselineau (New York: New York University
Press, 1965), p. 156. For a fuller discussion of
the same material, see Carl L. Anderson, The
Swedish Acceptance of American Literature (Phila-
delphia: University of Pennsylvania Press, 1957),
pp. 16-17, 21-23, 25-26, 64-67, 84-85, 98-100.

The first mention of Emily Dickinson in the
Swedish press was made by Margit Abenius in 1934.[4]
It is hardly surprising that a critic like Abenius
realized the quality of Emily Dickinson as early
as 1934, considering the high quality of her
criticism in general. In this article, Abenius
first compares Dickinson's letters to her poems,
saying that "Emily Dickinson's letters, generally
speaking, are not particularly fascinating. But
they have sentences like lightning, surprise
sentences that are bold, elementary, and defy
translation."[5] Abenius goes on to discuss at
great length the life of the poet, finding it
strange and fascinating. She calls Emily Dickinson "probably the greatest poet of America,"[6] an
independent judgment in a time period that had by
no means reached such a conclusion.

Abenius finds Emily Dickinson's knowledge of
both this world and of God surprising, seeing her
moving around in her particular heaven in an
"impish way, well at home."[7] Abenius writes:
"Polite little archangels cover their faces when
Jehovah passes by and seraphs swing their snow-
white hats. With a round and steady gaze, the

Sigmund Skard, in his American Studies in Europe:
Their History and Present Organization (Philadelphia: University of Pennsylvania Press, 1958), II,
439-41, discusses the same Swedish-American relationship, stressing a historical viewpoint that
complements Åhnebrink and Anderson.

[4]Margit Abenius, "Emily Dickinson," Bonniers
Litterära Magasin, 7 (1934), 18-23.

[5]Abenius, p. 18.

[6]Abenius, p. 18.

[7]Abenius, p. 21.

little person watches the procession of angels."[8]
It is obvious, remarks Abenius, that Dickinson
finds the angels rather bored in heaven, what with
every day being Sunday and the Holy Ghost constantly around, watch in hand. Furthermore, the poet
sees Jehovah as stingy, apart from being a swindler
and a burglar. He makes little people pay heavily
for one single sip of heaven.

Abenius finds great merit in those poems
treating death and concludes that "as a writer
mainly concerned with death she [Dickinson] ranks
among the foremost in the world."[9] Abenius also
has high praise for Emily Dickinson's love poetry.
She finds that Dickinson catches the reactions of
the nerves and the human organism in bold and
totally modern analogies; she believes that the
use of the past tense and of distance in the love
poetry produces a specific mixture of warmth and
rational thinking, of hot color and jarring loose
ends.

Abenius sees three specific types of Dickinsonian poetry. First, there is the elliptic,
quick, and absurd quality corresponding to her
penetrating lawyer's intellect, such as can be
seen in "I never saw a Moor." The second type is
stormy and electric, as in the poems dealing with
"the potential of nature." Abenius does not explain exactly what she means by "potential of
nature" and she mentions no poems as examples of
this second group. The third group consists of
poems dealing with the bat, the train, or the
balloon--this part of Dickinson's poetry is a
phenomenon of magic, concludes Abenius.

Ten years would pass before Abenius turned
again to Dickinson, this time to include her 1934
essay in a collection of literary criticism. Before that date and still in the thirties, two

[8]Abenius, p. 21.

[9]Abenius, p. 22.

8

other pioneers in poetry criticism, Erik Blomberg
and Johannes Edfelt, came out with translations as
well as more criticism. It is notable, although
in no way surprising, that it is the poets themselves who were the first to publish on Emily
Dickinson in Sweden. Apart from the perceptive
Abenius, no one in Sweden wrote on Dickinson before Blomberg in 1936 published translations of
three poems. The first poems translated into
Swedish were "Avsked" ["My life closed twice"];
"För skönhet dog jag" ["I died for Beauty"]; and
"I sina blå alabasterkamrar" ["Safe in their
Alabaster Chambers"].[10]

In 1941, Johannes Edfelt, renowned poet and
member of The Eighteen, wrote a long review-
article on Emily Dickinson.[11] This article was
entitled "Detta var en poet" ["This Was a Poet"]
after Whicher's book, which he briefly praises
before going on to Emily Dickinson's poetry itself. The poetry of this genius, as Edfelt calls
Dickinson, won unusually loyal supporters even as
early as the 1890's; strangely enough, Encyclopaedia Britannica does not mention her even in the
1930's, a fact which Edfelt finds surprising.[12]
At this time [in the 1940's], Edfelt writes, there
would be few critics in America or elsewhere who
would not consider Emily Dickinson probably the
best American poet. It is clear, Edfelt continues,
that she is an innovator and a poetic phenomenon
who was far ahead of her time.[13] "Nothing wrong
with Poe and Whitman, but this strange and en-

[10]Erik Blomberg, "Emily Dickinson: Tre
dikter" ["Emily Dickinson: Three Poems"],
Bonniers Litterära Magasin, 9 (1936), 597-98.

[11]Johannes Edfelt, "Detta var en poet,"
Dagens Nyheter, April 4, 1941, p. 5.

[12]Cf. Nordisk Familjebok, p. 5 of this chapter.

[13]Edfelt, p. 5.

9

chanting product of New England and of the nineteenth century speaks more intimately and directly
to a modern reader."[14] He finds the poems sensitive and bold in their complexity and branching-
out. "Many poets of today seem outdated in comparison with this poet."[15] American poetry, he
says, was in danger at this time, stiff in its
cliches, and Dickinson's poetry, especially her
nature poems, rescued America from this danger.
She is also the only American poet during this
century, he concludes, who manages to vary the
theme of love. She developed into a livskonstnär
("one who lives wisely") in the deepest sense:
revealing the pride, the independence, the heroism
in every situation, the subtle love of nature.
Helping to create this image of the livskonstnär
are her multi-faceted humor, her esprit, and her
good common sense. Edfelt, like Abenius before
him, pays tribute to the mixture of respect,
irony, and humor that is typical of her treatment
of religion. Edfelt concludes that her poetry is
a strange and wonderful mixture of bold analogies
and metaphors.[16]

In 1942, Artur Lundkvist, left-oriented
novelist, essayist, and critic, published Diktare
och Avslöjare i Amerikas Moderna Litteratur [Poets
and Revealers in the Modern Literature of
America].[17] In the preface, Lundkvist writes that
his intention is to give a complete picture of
American literature after 1890. Of the 120
writers dealt with, all should be of interest to

[14]Edfelt, p. 5.

[15]Edfelt, p. 5.

[16]Edfelt, p. 5.

[17]Artur Lundkvist, Diktare och Avslöjare i
Amerikas Moderna Litteratur (Stockholm: Kooperativa förbundets bokförlag, 1942). Lundkvist is
a member of The Eighteen.

the public, he says.[18] Particularly outstanding is one of the first chapters called "Realismens framväxt" ["The Growth of Realism"], where Lundkvist interprets Puritan New England. At the end of the period, he says, all that was left of the New England culture was "empty respectability and a shallow and hardened moralism and the earlier passion for reform had now become sentimental charity."[19] It was in this milieu of moral and social conventions that Emily Dickinson was born, a milieu that she revolted against in her poetry but that she did not free herself from in real life.

In the chapter called "Den nya lyriken" ["The New Poetry"], Lundkvist treats five poets, the most important of whom is Whitman, Lundkvist maintains.[20] But he finds Emily Dickinson of some importance, and he does not find that importance in any sense derivative. He observes that although she wrote about private matters, her poetry is not really for herself but for everyone. Brief and nonchalant and extremely compressed, her poetry is composed of a series of explosions, cool and passionate at the same time. Her motifs are those of the loner: God, love, death, eternity, and elementary nature. Her imagination fathoms everything; yet, Lundkvist concludes that she is hardly a first-rate poet. To the new poetry of America she has probably contributed little, other than presenting a poetry devoid of all form. This is the way the critical Lundkvist winds up his evaluation of Emily Dickinson.[21]

Three years after his first article on Dick-

[18]Lundkvist, p. i.

[19]Lundkvist, p. 11.

[20]Lundkvist, p. 52.

[21]Lundkvist, p. 54.

11

inson, Johannes Edfelt in 1944 translated "Molnig dag" and "Stamtavla" ["The Sky is low--the Clouds are mean" and "The pedigree of Honey"].[22] As mentioned before, Margit Abenius in the same year republished her 1934 article in a collection of criticism, Kontakter [Contacts].[23] At this time, Abenius had an even higher position among Swedish critics. Erik Lindegren, poet, critic, and later elected a member of The Eighteen, wrote a respectful and sympathetic review-article on her essay collection. It is his opinion that among the most durable of her essays are the ones on Emily Dickinson and Birger Sjöberg.[24] Abenius is concerned with "the independent soul," Lindegren says, the ambivalent and fragmentary.[25]

In 1946, Olov Lagercrantz wrote in a publication preview[26] in Svenska Dagbladet that "America

[22]Johannes Edfelt, "Två dikter av Emily Dickinson" ["Two Poems by Emily Dickinson"], Ord och Bild, [n.v.] (1944), p. 583. Ord och Bild has been defunct for many years; it was a prestigious literary magazine which fell victim to the changing economy of newspapers everywhere. Later, when the magazine was bound by year, the pages containing volume numbers, etc., were removed to save space. Now, the only information left is that of year and pages.

[23]Margit Abenius, Kontakter (Stockholm: Bonniers, 1944), pp. 93-104.

[24]Birger Sjöberg was an early twentieth-century poet, a lyricist, and a composer. His most famous collection of poetry set to music is Fridas visor [Frida's Songs].

[25]Erik Lindegren, "Den osynlige läsaren" ["The Invisible Reader"], Bonniers Litterära Magasin, 17 (1944), 903-05.

[26]A "publication preview" is the present writer's term for the Swedish term blänkare

enjoyed a first-rate sensation last spring when
666 hitherto unknown poems by Emily Dickinson were
published as a book."[27] The first copy reached
Sweden last week, he continues, and remarks that
one touches the pages much as one would an unknown
collection of poetry by Tegnér[28] or Fröding.[29]
Lagercrantz considers the new poems as good as any
previously published ones.

Ord och Bild, one of the most prestigious
Swedish literary magazines, in 1946 published a
long article about Emily Dickinson starting with
a brief review of Todd-Bingham's Bolts of Melody.[30]

["blinker"]. It can "blink" at several things;
for example, a very recent publication, a coming
review, and it can even come close to an advertise-
ment. The purpose of a "publication preview" is
most often to alert the readers of things to come;
when dealing with things past, it can resemble a
review of any cultural event--the publication of a
book or a live performance.

[27]Olov Lagercrantz, [no title; publication
preview], Svenska Dagbladet, April 8, 1946, p. 8.
The book referred to is presumably Mabel Loomis
Todd and Millicent Todd Bingham, eds., Bolts of
Melody: New Poems of Emily Dickinson (New York:
Harper and Brothers, 1945).

[28]The Swedish poet laureate par excellence;
nineteenth-century poet, critic, and bishop
(1782-1846).

[29]For Fröding, see the first page of this
chapter.

[30]Ebba Lindqvist, "Emily Dickinson efter många
år" ["Emily Dickinson after Many Years], Ord
och Bild, [n.v.] (1946), pp. 581-85. The reference is to Mabel Loomis Todd and Millicent Todd
Bingham, eds., Bolts of Melody: New Poems of Emily
Dickinson (New York: Harper and Brothers, 1945).

13

In the article, Ebba Lindqvist writes that the sensation of finding new poems by Emily Dickinson is comparable to finding new Shakespeare dramas. According to Lindqvist, together with Emily Brontë, Emily Dickinson is the greatest English-speaking poet the world has produced. The critic finds that the Emily of the new collection of poetry is the same as we have known before: the same monologues or dialogues, the same range of subject matter, from the little worm to God, the same intense love of excitement, the same awe of life itself. If there is anything new it has to be the poems concerning fame.[31] It has often been said, Lindqvist continues, that Emily Dickinson had no interest in "fame," but she finds this view mistaken, judging from the number of poems treating the subject.[32] Some of the poems are particularly intense, for instance the ones inspired by the Civil War. It is obvious that the Civil War deeply influenced Emily Dickinson. According to the poet, the knowledge that others also suffer is of no help to the separate individual.[33]

Lindqvist also discusses the psychological implications of the relationships within the Dickinson family. She concludes that in spite of the fact that Emily Dickinson knew relatively few people and never married, her mind was able to "encompass a universe" and grasp a wide range of emotions.[34]

The years 1949 and 1950 are milestones in Dickinson criticism in Sweden. Ellen Löfmarck published her first article on Emily Dickinson in

[31]Lindqvist, p. 581.

[32]Lindqvist, pp. 581-82.

[33]Lindqvist, p. 582.

[34]Lindqvist, pp. 584-85.

1949.[35] In the same year, Erik Blomberg and
Johannes Edfelt published the very first collection of Emily Dickinson's poetry translated into
Swedish (including the three poems translated by
Blomberg in 1936).[36] In Europe in general and in
Scandinavia in particular, being translated has
always meant having arrivé. It is only after the
intellectual elite have accepted a foreign writer
that a publishing house considers translation of
foreign literature into the native language money
well spent. Consequently, one may judge Emily
Dickinson well established in Sweden as of 1949.

In her article, "Den ensamma damen från
Amherst" ["The Lonely Lady from Amherst"], Ellen
Löfmarck writes that Emily Dickinson is an even
more astonishing phenomenon now [1949] than she
must have seemed to her contemporaries. It is
amazing, Löfmarck continues, how somebody who knew
so few people can know--people.[37] Her eye is the
eye of the microscope, but she concentrates only
on details eternally human."[38] The changing
quality of life is of less interest than the timeless. Death and love are the two central themes
in Emily Dickinson's poetry, Löfmarck maintains.
Löfmarck evaluates Emily Dickinson as "a poetic
genius and a fascinating paradox" but, at the same
time, finds her "inconsistent and whimsical," and
a poet not altogether free from sentimentality and
not altogether great. Löfmarck devotes a good
part of her article to the life of Emily Dickinson,
the poet who left behind her "the greatest poetic

[35]Ellen Löfmarck, "Den ensamma damen från
Amherst," Idun, 23 (June 1949), 8, 9, 18.

[36]Erik Blomberg and Johannes Edfelt, Dikter
[Poems] (Stockholm: Wahlström och Widstrand, 1949).

[37]Löfmarck, pp. 8, 9.

[38]Löfmarck, p. 9.

treasure of America."[39]   In all probability,
Löfmarck concludes, the Dickinson poems that we
now have are the last ones.[40]

Also in 1949, four small publication previews
appeared. In Stockholms-Tidningen, an anonymous
critic briefly notes the fact that Inger Hagerup
[of Norway] has published translations of and comments on Emily Dickinson's poetry, and goes on to
observe that in Sweden two full-length books will
shortly appear, one by Blomberg and Edfelt, and
one by Ellen Löfmarck.[41]

In the left-oriented Morgon-Tidningen, one
month later, Vg. [signature] announces that two
exquisite volumes of translated poetry have just
been published--one the poems of Heinrich Heine,
the other the poems of Emily Dickinson. The two
poets have much in common, he concludes: they made
as much use of their losses in life as of their
victories. The Emily Dickinson book is the
Blomberg-Edfelt collection of translations.[42]

In Stockholms-Tidningen, Anders Österling
writes a publication preview that is also a brief
review of the Blomberg-Edfelt publication. This
spinster of genius [Emily Dickinson] from Amherst,
Massachusetts, who in her lonely hours filled her
desk drawers with bold thoughts and outstanding

[39]Löfmarck, p. 9.

[40]At the time Löfmarck was writing, only
forty-one poems remained to be published for the
first time. See Thomas H. Johnson, ed., The Poems
of Emily Dickinson (Cambridge, Mass.: The Belknap
Press of Harvard University Press, 1955), I, Lx.

[41][no title; publication preview], Stockholms-Tidningen, September 19, 1949, p. 5.

[42]Vg., [no title; publication preview],
Morgon-Tidningen, October 24, 1949, p. 5.

impromptus is one of the phenomena of world literature," says Österling.[43] There are good reasons,
Österling maintains, for getting tired of the format of Dickinson's poetry, namely if one reads too
much of it; reading her poetry in selection does
her more justice. "The two translators show a
fine insight into the precise quality of the poetess." Blomberg's interpretation of "Success is
counted sweetest" all but equals the original,
Österling argues, and he concludes the preview by
quoting Blomberg's translation of that poem.

In Sydsvenska Dagbladet Snällposten, H. Dhe
[signature of Hans Dhejne] alerts the readers of
the biggest newspaper south of Göteborg [Gothen-
burg] to the appearance of the Blomberg-Edfelt
book, praising in particular the excellence of
Yngve Berg's illustrations.[44] Two of the best
interpreters of foreign poetry are Blomberg and
Edfelt, Dhejne maintains. Even in as difficult a

[43]Anders Österling, [no title; publication
preview], Stockholms-Tidningen, October 31, 1949,
p. 5.

[44]Hans Dhejne, [no title; publication pre-
view], Sydsvenska Dagbladet Snällposten, December
14, 1949, [C.A.]. This article comes from Klippar-
kivet [The Clipping Archive, i.e., C.A.], Sigtuna,
Sweden. For common-sense reasons, the Archive,
like other scholarly Swedish institutions, does
not give page numbers for daily newspapers. Swedish daily newspapers contain very few pages. There
is not much advertising and recurring topics are
normally to be found on the same pages each day.
Thus, news in general, political news in particular, is to be found on the first 3-5 pages. "The
cultural pages" are always to be found in the middle. Often "the cultural pages" have a name in
addition to a page number. So, for instance,
Östgöta Correspondenten has its "Regnbågen" ["The
Rainbow"] as exemplified in footnotes 52 and 59-61
of this chapter. Similarly, Hufvudstadsbladet in

17

case as that of transposing the poetry of Emily
Dickinson, they have managed to maintain the high
level of quality that their readers are accustomed to.

Edfelt and Blomberg published their translations at the end of the year, all in all twenty-
eight.[45] It is a small selection indeed, but the
poems are carefully chosen. Among them are some
that will appear in different translations again
and again, such as "Apparently with no surprise";
"I died for Beauty"; and "Safe in their Alabaster
Chambers."[46]

Ellen Löfmarck's Emily Dickinson was well-

Helsingfors has its "Lördagsextra" ["Saturday Ex-
tras"] (see footnote 156). Many of the page numbers that were not supplied by the Clipping Archive have been obtained by other means, such as
microfilms. In some instances there are no microfilms in existence, for example in the case of
older and now defunct daily newspapers.

[45]Cf. footnote 36.

[46]Among these poems, translations of the
following are to be found: "The rainbow never
tells me"; "In lands I never saw--they say"; "The
Sky is low--the Clouds are mean"; "I know that He
exists"; "Heart! We will forget him!"; "My life
closed twice before its close"; "Hope is a subtle
Glutton"; "I asked no other thing"; "The Heart
asks Pleasure--first"; "Surgeons must be very
careful"; "The Brain--is wider than the Sky";
"Success is counted sweetest"; "If I should'nt be
alive"; "What Inn is this"; "To fight aloud, is
very brave"; "I sing to use the Waiting"; "I like
a look of Agony"; and "I never saw a Moor."

timed and immediately received much attention.[47]
The first sixty-six pages consist of critical
material and the remainder of the book is devoted
to fifty-nine translated poems. For some years
after the publication of this book, Löfmarck remained the great name in Dickinson criticism in
Sweden. Her reputation rested more on competence
in writing about Dickinson than on the translations themselves, an area where she had to compete
with three giants in the literary world, namely
Blomberg, Edfelt, and, later on, Lars von Haar-
man.[48] The reader of Löfmarck's book first gets a
detailed description of the poet's background and
family situation. Löfmarck feels that it was un-
fortunate that "the best poetry produced in America"[49] was left to the whims of Lavinia Dickinson,
finding Lavinia lacking both intuition and a pioneering spirit. Löfmarck goes on to compare Emily
Dickinson to the sleeping beauty in the sense that
it took decades for the world to put her on the
level where she belongs.[50]

Knut Jaensson, a well-known literary critic
in Sweden, contributed to the new rush of Dickin-

[47]Ellen Löfmarck, Emily Dickinson (Stockholm:
Bröderna Lagerström, 1950). Subsequent references
to this book will be cited as Löfmarck, ED.

[48]In all fairness, one can also speculate as
to whether the well-publicized fact that Löfmarck
was a dentist and that she did not wear the union
label of a Ph.D. might have made her translations
more vulnerable to critical neglect. The same
might be true in the case of Haartman, whose Ph.D.
is in Zoology. To the mind of the present writer,
however, the very fact that Dickinson attracted
the attention of a wide range of different person-
alities is the ultimate tribute to her art.

[49]Löfmarck, ED, p. 38.

[50]Löfmarck, ED, pp. 33-54.

son criticism an article called "En postum diktarbana" ["The Posthumous Career of a Poet"].[51] He
compares Emily Dickinson to the Swedish poet Stagnelius[52] in the sense that all of their poetry
sprang from a necessity to sacrifice in life.[53]
Jaensson does not qualify his admiration for Emily
Dickinson. It is true, he says, that life and
death may have been of equal importance to other
poets, but hardly anyone felt the reality of the
"alabaster chambers" as intensely as Emily Dickinson. He believes that the aphoristic quality of
her verse contributes to its sense of timelessness.[54]

The conservative Östgöta Correspondenten the
same year published an unsigned article called
"Emily Dickinson--amerikansk klassiker" ["Emily
Dickinson--An American Classic"].[55] The article,
generally speaking, is a statement concerning the
status that Emily Dickinson had reached. Now,
fifty years after her death, she has to be considered the greatest of the nineteenth-century
American poets. The unknown critic considers the
main reason for Emily Dickinson's superiority to
be her linguistic instinct and vitality.

[51]Knut Jaensson, "En postum diktarbana,"
Dagens Nyheter, March 20, 1950, p. 5.

[52]Swedish romantic poet who wrote about
nature and the mystery of life in general in the
nineteenth century.

[53]Jaensson, p. 5.

[54]Jaensson, p. 5.

[55]"Emily Dickinson--amerikansk klassiker,"
Östgöta Correspondenten, July 15, 1950, p. Regn-
bågen 2. Probably the article was written by
F.Ch. [signature of Stina Ridderstad] who, at
other times, wrote on literature in Östgöta
Correspondenten.

Lgn. [signature of Emil Liedgren] published
"Ett enda glas av himlen" ["One Single Glass of
Heaven"] in Västmanlands Läns Tidning, one of the
oldest and best known newspapers in Sweden.[56]
Liedgren observes that Dickinson obviously wrote
because she had a need to express herself and not
with a view toward publication or fame. He agrees
with almost every critic that love and death are
the core of her world and thinking. Possibly even
more enchanting he finds her poems about summer
and nature in general in which she uses nature as
a metaphor for the sacred. Liedgren says that the
readers [of VLT] would probably prefer to read the
poet in English despite the fact that Löfmarck's
book has kept many of the qualities of the original.[57]

The rush of Emily Dickinson criticism was
only beginning. In March, 1950, F.Ch. [signature
of Stina Ridderstad] published an article in
Östgöta Correspondenten. It, too, starts out as
a review of Löfmarck but the article quickly turns
into an analysis of the poetry itself.[58] Some of
Ridderstad's views are refreshingly different from
those of other critics. She suggests that Emily
Dickinson's isolation prompted her to live in "a
world filled with visions, impressions, and
thoughts,"[59] intensifying passion and pain and
forcing her to express herself in strange, concentrated, and sharp poems. Like other critics,
Ridderstad assumes that the last Dickinson poem

[56]Emil Liedgren, "Ett enda glas av himlen,"
Västmanlands Läns Tidning, March 22, 1950, p. 5.
Professor Liedgren holds a doctorate in Theology.

[57]Liedgren, p. 5.

[58]Stina Ridderstad, "En klassisk amerikansk
skaldinna" ["A Classic American Poetess"], Östgöta
Correspondenten, March 24, 1950, Regnbågen p. 2.

[59]Ridderstad, Regnbågen p. 2.

has been published. Attempting to grasp the
source of Dickinson's poetic gift, Ridderstad observes that although it is difficult to pinpoint
its exact nature, one thing is certain: whether
the poems are the result of an actual life experience or imagination, they are rendered in the best
form possible. Dickinson says what she wants to
say and nothing else. This concentration is the
gift of the first-rate artist, Ridderstad concludes.[60]

In Stockholms-Tidningen, Anders Österling
published "Emily Dickinson på svenska" ["Emily
Dickinson in Swedish"].[61] This article, like many
others, starts out as a brief review of both the
Blomberg-Edfelt collection of poetry and Löfmarck's
book and then becomes an essay on Dickinson. Emily
Dickinson, Österling says, is herself a symbol of
the loneliness that grows out of hurt feelings.
She never tired of finding the right expression
corresponding to her inner experience. Yet, she
could be quite artificial when she felt vulnerable,
Österling says.

Later in the article, Österling refers to the
667 poems unearthed by Todd-Bingham in 1929. He
fears that the great quantity of her poetic output
may carry the built-in danger of monotony and
mediocrity in a sizable number of the less successful poems. Still, her best poetry is "alive
and unforgettable."[62] Both her technique and content, Österling continues, had left conventions
far behind. Although God, love, and eternity were
her themes, as in the case of the classics, her
mind had a light and teasing bend, a girlish

[60]Ridderstad, Regnbågen p. 2.

[61]Anders Österling, "Emily Dickinson på
svenska," Stockholms-Tidningen, March 27, 1950,
p. 4.

[62]Österling, p. 4.

euphoria and playfulness that only became more intense as she faced serious questions. Although
critics have called Emily Dickinson primitive,
particularly with regard to her grammar, Österling
finds her word economy rather sophisticated.
Österling compares Dickinson to Heine: "She walk-
ed in her garden . . . and caught metaphysical
paradoxes like butterflies."[63] He also compares
her to another literary champion for individual
freedom, women's freedom in particular, the Swedish writer Fredrika Bremer, who visited Massachusetts and moved in the social circles of Boston at
the same time that Emily Dickinson corresponded
with Colonel Higginson. The two women never met,
but to a Swede, familiar with both biographies,
the parallel is striking. Both lived in a time
when women were supposed to develop social skills
rather than satisfy intellectual passions. In
addition, both had dominating fathers and managed
to add writing to their daily household chores.

At the end of the article, Österling again
returns to Löfmarck's translations (not her critical comments), only to judge them mediocre. His
comments are perhaps not surprising in view of the
fact that he himself was a first-rate poet and
that Löfmarck's poems have to be compared to the
Blomberg-Edfelt collection of competent translations. Later on, Lars von Haartman was to be a
worthy competitor for the title of best Emily
Dickinson translator into Swedish.

In the prestigious "Göteborgs Handels-och
Sjöfartstidning, Ebba Lindqvist published "Emily
Dickinson presenteras" ["Presenting Emily Dickinson"].[64] The title refers to Löfmarck's book and,
on the whole, Lindqvist agrees with Österling that

[63]Österling, p. 4.

[64]Ebba Lindqvist, "Emily Dickinson presenteras," Göteborgs Handels-och Sjöfartstidning,
April 13, 1960, p. 3. Subsequent references to
this article will be cited as "ED presenteras."

Löfmarck's translations have lost much of the
Dickinson originality. Lindqvist then devotes
most of her article to Dickinson herself, her life
and poetry. Dickinson's strength, according to
Lindqvist, was her love of nature, but even more,
it was her unusual sense of humor and disregard
for conventions in general. She mastered her
primary tool, language, as few have done. If,
Lindqvist concludes, the rhyme is not the expected
one, it is only because she desired an effect more
intense, more surprising, and less trivial.[65]

K.-E.H. [signature] wrote a publication preview called "The Amherst nun" [sic], in Upsala Nya
Tidning.[66] The tone of the preview is light and
one of the points made is the following: do not
publish before you are dead and fame will be yours.
But K.-E.H. admits that however "bitter" Emily
Dickinson's poetry might be, it never lacks grace
and vitality.

In Samtid och Framtid, Professor Carl Fehrman
published "Emily Dickinson på svenska" ["Emily
Dickinson in Swedish"].[67] Again, this is an article that starts out as a brief review of Löfmarck's
book but almost immediately turns into an analysis
of the Dickinson poetry itself. Fehrman interestingly compares Emily Dickinson to Edith Södergran,
a twentieth-century Swedish-speaking poet. He
sees them both as loners who, behind the narrow
fence of their limited life experiences, managed
to grasp eternity. The very fact that they were
lonely helped them to keep their respective dream-
worlds. Both of them were contemporaries of

[65]Lindqvist, "ED presenteras," p. 3.

[66]K-E.H., "The Amherst nun," Upsala Nya
Tidning, April 25, 1950, p. 7.

[67]Carl Fehrman, "Emily Dickinson på svenska,"
Samtid och Framtid, 5 (May 1950), 312-13.

posterity, rather than of their own life time.[68]
Emily Dickinson, Fehrman concludes, is the great
innovator of American poetry mainly because of her
lack of formal linguistic conventions.

Even the evening newspaper Afton-Tidningen,
traditionally less culturally oriented than the
morning papers, had a long review-article by Hans
Levander, "Gärdsmygen från Amherst" ["The Wren
from Amherst"].[69] The review is rather critical
of Löfmarck's translations but almost all of the
article is devoted to Emily Dickinson herself.
Her poetic genius allowed her to write poetry
about love without much actual experience to guide
her; no romantic legend is necessary for the
reader to believe in her love poetry, writes
Levander. Her linguistic ability leaves the
reader breathless; her unexpected juxtapositions,
her often shocking vocabulary, a sudden change in
rhythm and her shy wittiness, all of this may re-
mind one of Birger Sjöberg.[70] It requires no
great profundity, Levander continues, to regard
Dickinson as a poet who anticipated almost every
aspect that we now consider typical of modern
poetry.

[68]Haartman (see footnote 2) finds most comparisons between these two poets strained. For
one thing, Södergran ought to be dressed all in
red, corresponding to Dickinson's white. The red
color would suit the "overheated" quality of
Södergran whom Haartman places below Dickinson.
(Letter received from Lars von Haartman, 7 September 1977).

[69]Hans Levander, "Gärdsmygen från Amherst,"
Afton-Tidningen, May 16, 1950, pp. 2-3. Among
other things, Dr. Levander has written on Thomas
Mann.

[70]For Sjöberg, see the first page of this
chapter and footnote 24.

Stig Carlson, left-oriented critic, published
"Ett amerikanskt diktaröde" ["The Fate of an American Poet"] in Morgon-Tidningen.[71] Carlson writes
that ever since Dickinson's break-through in the
United States in the early twenties, she has been
the object of a kind of cult-worship that hardly
anyone is served by. He puts most of the blame on
Mrs. Bianchi but also on critics all around the
world who have engaged in "a panting and pathetic worship."[72] The simple truth is, Carlson
maintains, that Dickinson had an unusual sense of
the value of words and that she was a highly sug-
gestible creature who, like a sleepwalker, stum-
bled on instinctively correct interpretations of
people and problems. Carlson feels that Dickinson's knowledge of death was intimate and minute
and that the poetry dealing with death is her
best. He argues that Dickinson without exception
considered death as a friend, not a cruel enemy--
rather a mild and sympathetic male friend. He
considers her intense curiosity about death
natural and not the eccentric obsession that it
has seemed to many critics. At the end of his
article, Carlson's tone becomes even more critical.
One should not forget, he says, that Emily Dickinson is often sentimental. "Her lack of involve-
ment in any deeper sense . . . [makes] the air
around her poetry seem rather thin and transpar-
ent."[73] Carlson's article remains one of the more
adversely critical in Swedish criticism.

Still in the landmark year of 1950, Olov
Lagercrantz published a long article entitled "Om
Emily Dickinson" ["About Emily Dickinson"].[74] The

[71]Stig Carlson, "Ett amerikanskt diktaröde,"
Morgon-Tidningen, June 3, 1950, p. 4.

[72]Carlson, p. 4.

[73]Carlson, p. 4.

[74]Olov Lagercrantz, "Om Emily Dickinson,"
Svenska Dagbladet, June 13, 1950, p. 7.

title seems to refer to the fact that this article, unlike his previous publication, deals less directly with the poetry itself; rather, he attempts an evaluation of the status of Emily Dickinson in Sweden at this particular point. Now, Lagercrantz maintains, one can state for the first time that Emily Dickinson is generally known in Sweden; in fact, so much has been written about her that one may even question whether her poetry, excellent as it is, merits all of this attention. Lagercrantz devotes a good part of the article to comparisons; a comparison between Löfmarck as a critic and as a translator, between Löfmarck as translator on one hand and Blomberg and Edfelt on the other. Löfmarck as a critic gets a high rating by Lagercrantz, an opinion shared by other critics. On the other hand, Lagercrantz calls Löfmarck's translations "often unsuccessful," particularly when compared to those of Blomberg and Edfelt. He considers both of these poets first-rate translators and particularly mentions Blomberg's version of "Success is counted sweetest" as a near-perfect translation, an opinion which he shares with Österling.[75] As a summary of the state of Dickinson criticism and translations, the effort is important. Of even more interest, though, is Lagercrantz' frame of reference, clearly stated in the first part of the article. The lover of poetry who has yet to make the acquaintance of Dickinson has a great pleasure before him, he says. She is not a poet who appeals to the "literary gourmets" alone, but to everyone, Lagercrantz emphatically states.

Svenska Dagbladet, a month later, carried a brief but flattering publication preview by V.N. [signature of Ven Nyberg]. The preview itself regards the upcoming definitive edition of Dickinson's poems by Thomas Johnson. Typical of her comments is the following: "Finally she [Dickinson] has been identified as the greatest woman

[75]See footnote 43.

poet of our time."[76]

"Främsta skaldinnan i USA" ["The Foremost
Poetess of the United States"] was the title of
still another 1950 article by J.L. [signature of
John Landquist].[77] There seems to be a growing
sentiment that Emily Dickinson may be the greatest
poet America ever produced, Professor Landquist
states. He finds her poetry expressing a lonely
person's attitude toward living, the attitude of
a person accustomed to sacrifices. He sees her
images as naive and exquisite at the same time.
Landquist interestingly compares Dickinson's attitude toward the "dangerous and impish" adventure
of living to the world-view of the German artist,
Albrecht Dürer.

The Landquist article marks the end of 1950,
as far as Swedish Dickinson criticism is concerned. In 1951, Ellen Löfmarck published an article
on "Emily Dickinsons brev" ["Emily Dickinson's
Letters"].[78] Löfmarck still puts emphasis on her
former opinion that Dickinson first of all is a
poet, but, she adds, "the elusively sheer voice
that is hers alone grabs the reader as inevitably
as does the voice of her poetry."[79] The critic's

[76]Ven Nyberg, [no title; publication preview],
Svenska Dagbladet, July 10, 1950, p. 5.

[77]John Landquist, "Främsta skaldinnan i USA,
Afton-Bladet, July 25, 1950, p. 4.

[78]Ellen Löfmarck, "Emily Dickinsons brev,"
Dagens Nyheter, June 18, 1951, p. 2. Subsequent
references to this article will be cited as "EDs
brev." The edition of Dickinson's letters referred to is Mabel Loomis Todd, ed., Letters of
Emily Dickinson (Cleveland: World Publishing
Company, 1951).

[79]Löfmarck, "EDs brev," p. 2.

approach to Dickinson's writing, whether poetry or prose, should be the same, because the problems are the same, Löfmarck continues. Who is to say, she concludes, where the distinction lies between the naively pathetic and the sublimely poetic; one only knows that the style of Dickinson's writing is beyond reproach, especially that of her death poetry.

In 1951, Afton-Bladet carried an anonymous publication preview announcing Rebecca Patterson's The Riddle of Emily Dickinson.[80] The preview does not identify Patterson's thesis; it only hints at a "new and sensational solution to the problem of Emily Dickinson's secret love."

Johannes Edfelt, for the first time since his collaboration with Blomberg in 1949, again turned to Emily Dickinson in 1951.[81] His article was entitled "Emily Dickinson och dr. Holland" ["Emily Dickinson and Dr. Holland"]. Despite the fact, Edfelt says, that Dickinson's poetic sensibility and linguistic boldness must have been beyond Dr. and Mrs. Holland, Emily Dickinson felt close enough to them to give openly of her secretive and elusive personality. Her letters give equally good examples of the surprising metaphors that she was a master of in poetry.[82] Her letters often show the same condensed, epigrammatic form found in her poetry. Even the teasing way of handling serious matters, her courage, and her warmth of heart remain the same, whether in poetry or prose, concludes Edfelt.

[80] [no title; publication preview], Afton-Bladet, September 28, 1951, p. 4.

[81] Johannes Edfelt, "Emily Dickinson och dr. Holland," Dagens Nyheter, October 25, 1951, p. 4.

[82] Here Edfelt differs from Abenius; see footnote 5 of this chapter.

As mentioned before, <u>Afton-Bladet</u> had carried a publication preview of Patterson's forthcoming book. In <u>Dagens Nyheter</u>, Ellen Löfmarck turned to a discussion of Emily Dickinson's suggested lesbianism. The article first contains a brief review of Patterson's book,[83] and returns to the review at the end of the article. The middle part of the article is devoted to comments on various possibilities regarding the object of Dickinson's affections. The style of this section of the article is light: could it really have been the "boring" Wadsworth or perhaps the not overly perceptive Higginson? Kate? Löfmarck implies that this kind of source-hunting is trivial. The article is called "Gåtan Emily Dickinson" ["The Riddle of Emily Dickinson"]. Löfmarck's attitude toward Patterson's book is balanced. She says that even though she herself had been curious about a certain Kate when her name appeared in Dickinson's letters, it had never occurred to her that the letters were love letters. It is hardly as a profound psychologist, but rather as someone with the mentality of "an American star reporter"[84] that Patterson has solved the riddle of Emily Dickinson. On the other hand, Löfmarck concludes, Patterson has really done more than just solve a riddle. "With all its weaknesses, <u>The Riddle of Emily Dickinson</u> is one of the most outstanding contributions to Dickinson scholarship,"[85] an opinion not shared by many critics.

[83]Ellen Löfmarck, "Gåtan Emily Dickinson," <u>Dagens Nyheter</u>, May 11, 1952, p. 4. Subsequent references to this article will be cited as "Gåtan ED." The edition of letters that prompted this article is Theodora Ward, ed., <u>Emily Dickinson's Letters to Dr. and Mrs. Josiah Gilbert Holland</u> (Cambridge, Mass.: Harvard University Press, 1951).

[84]Löfmarck, "Gåtan ED," p. 4.

[85]Löfmarck, "Gåtan ED," p. 4.

Birger Christoffersson, in "Emily Dickinsons teknik" ["Emily Dickinson's Technique"], compares her linguistic "frugality" and "simplicity" to the style of Harry Martinson.[86] Dickinson, Christoffersson maintains, is not indebted to the past; instead, her poetry stretches out toward the next century. She anticipated Kafka just as obviously as the Swedish literature of the forties followed in his footsteps, Christoffersson concludes his article.

For the next two years, Emily Dickinson was not mentioned in the Swedish press. Curiously, it was again Christoffersson who, in 1955, wrote "Emily Dickinsons hemlighet" ["Emily Dickinson's Secret"].[87] In this article, Christoffersson first summarizes what too many critics, according to him, have seen in Emily Dickinson: the "angel-like" quality. Instead, he says, Rebecca Patterson's suggestion that Emily loved a woman called Kate seems realistic; many poems are suddenly easier to understand. What used to be "angel-like" is now "passionate." What used to make the reader think of Blake now makes him think of Sappho. Christoffersson concludes: "One can now say that every line of Dickinson's poetry has been invested with a secret tension."[88]

In an article, "Emily Dickinson och offent-

[86]Birger Christoffersson, "Emily Dickinsons teknik," Morgon-Tidningen, May 4, 1953, p. 3. Harry Martinson was a renowned Swedish poet and novelist and also a member of The Eighteen. He shared the Nobel Prize in Literature with Eyvind Johnson in 1974.

[87]Birger Christoffersson, "Emily Dickinsons hemlighet," Stockholms-Tidningen, January 17, 1955, p. 4. Subsequent references to this article will be cited as "EDs hemlighet."

[88]Christoffersson, "EDs hemlighet," p. 4.

ligheten" ["Emily Dickinson and Public Life"],
Ellen Löfmarck pays tribute to Thomas H. Johnson
and his two major publications on Emily Dickinson,
The Poems of Emily Dickinson and Emily Dickinson:
An Interpretive Biography.[89] Dickinson is now as
public as she will ever be, Löfmarck writes, and
fame is certainly hers.

Mm. [signature of Mats Molander],[90] in an
article called "Emily Dickinson" in Dagens Nyheter,
commented on a radio program by Ellen Löfmarck.[91]
The program itself seems to have had much the same
content as many articles by Löfmarck. Molander
goes on to write on what he sees as the core of
Dickinson; her isolation, which he considers
chosen rather than forced. It is this very isolation, Molander maintains, that gives her the insight into people and the power to look for what
is universal beyond what is personal. Above all,
it was her humility in confronting death, love,
and life itself, that made her great, he concludes.

In Stockholms-Tidningen, an anonymous critic
commented on another radio program, this one by
Christoffersson.[92] The main point that Christoffersson made during "this literary half-hour" was
that, in his opinion, no single life experience,
whether heterosexual or homosexual, whether deal-

[89]Ellen Löfmarck, "Emily Dickinson och offentligheten," Dagens Nyheter, May 26, 1956, p. 4.

[90]Mm. is the late Mats Molander whose literary criticism often dealt with cultural radio
programs. In Scandinavia, 30-60 minute radio
programs devoted to all aspects of art are an
almost daily feature.

[91]Mats Molander, "Emily Dickinson," Dagens
Nyheter, March 9, 1957, p. 10.

[92][no title; publication preview], Stockholms-
Tidningen, April 11, 1958, p. 13.

ing with death or other major problems, can explain the total sum of Dickinson's accomplishments. One has to accept a greatness such as hers in faith and gratitude; over-simplified interpretations will never suffice.

The above radio review-article marked the end of the decade in Swedish Dickinson criticism. It may seem curious in view of the fact that Johnson had made 1955 a major year for Dickinson scholarship that a relatively small number of articles were published between 1955 and 1960. The sixties, however, saw increasing quantities of high-quality scholarly work published.

In 1960, Löfmarck wrote a nostalgic article, "Resan till Amherst" ["The Journey to Amherst"], which deals exclusively with the physical milieu of the poet in her lifetime compared to the Amherst of today [1960].[93] Löfmarck undertook the long journey to America at a time when trips between continents were not so common as today and perhaps not considered a necessity for a literary critic to gather first-hand information. The value of the article lies mainly in the very fact that it constitutes a proof of a life-long devotion to Emily Dickinson on the part of the author. Löfmarck does not pretend to present any new material, merely to tell about her own joy in visiting Amherst in person.

Only five days later, Löfmarck published "Emily, ensamheten och Gud" ["Emily, Isolation, and God"], in the same newspaper.[94] The more one reads Emily Dickinson, Löfmarck writes, the more obvious the reasons for her self-imposed isolation

[93]Ellen Löfmarck, "Resan till Amherst," Dagens Nyheter, January 3, 1960, p. 4.

[94]Ellen Löfmarck, "Emily, ensamheten och Gud," Dagens Nyheter, January 8, 1960, p. 4.

seem.[95] Dickinson closed her door to the outside
world, not to escape the world, as some would have
it, but to conquer it, writes Löfmarck. To be
able to economize in words, she had to economize
in actual living. Why use more words, she continues, than were necessary and why do things that
were not necessary? She had lived a conventional
life for many years and knew the choice she was
making.

However, the intelligentsia was not alone at
this time in recognizing the value of Dickinson's
poetry. Nils Ekman, in Beklädnadsfolket, translated "Jag dog för skönheten" ["I died for
Beauty"].[96] The reason for including the translation in this type of magazine is not immediately
apparent. Beklädnadsfolket is a workers' trade
magazine, mostly geared to the garment workers.
The articles "surrounding" the unexplained Dickinson insert deal with the lack of quality material
and quality performance so common nowadays: the
prime example given regards the mediocre quality
of most radio programs.[97] Whatever the reason for
the inclusion of the poem in this magazine, it
constitutes a very special tribute to Dickinson,
expanding her audience to include not only intellectuals and academicians, but the general public
as well.

[95]Cf. Molander who also considered the isolation voluntary.

[96]Nils Ekman, "Jag dog för skönheten,"
Beklädnadsfolket, 8 (1961), 15. Nils Ekman has
also translated Garcia Lorca.

[97]Professor Thomas W. Ford has suggested that
the common denominator for both the poem and the
articles might be the thesis of this particular
Dickinson poem: beauty is truth, and truth is
beauty, in a Keatsian sense. This explanation
seems eminently sensible. (In private conversation, September 1977).

34

In 1961, Johannes Edfelt edited a volume called Världens bästa lyrik i urval [The World's Best Poetry in Selection].[98] Considering that the book virtually covers the globe, the fact that three Dickinson poems are included is important recognition.[99] Of particular interest is Edfelt's introduction which is as helpful as it is learned. Among other things, Edfelt gives a survey of what some of the foremost modern theoreticians have to say about the distinctions between poetry and other art forms. Edfelt pays particular tribute to Emil Staiger who, in his Grundbegriffe der Poetik [The Basic Properties of Poetry],[100] subtly characterizes poetry as "the art of loneliness," the art that is quietly poured into the reader. Contrary to this, prose "catches" the reader (a more visible action) and drama puts him in a state of acute suspension.[101] It is likely, then, that Edfelt and Staiger would both consider the circumstances of Emily Dickinson's private life a fertile situation for providing first-rate poetry.

[98]Johannes Edfelt, ed., Världens bästa lyrik i urval (Stockholm: Natur och Kultur, 1961). Subsequent references to this book will be cited as Lyrik.

[99]Edfelt, Lyrik, pp. 290-91. The three poems are "Alper" ["In lands I never saw"]; "I sina blå alabasterkamrar" ["Safe in their Alabaster Chambers"]; and "För skönhet dog jag" ["I died for Beauty"].

[100]Emil Staiger is a Swiss esthetician and professor of 19th century German Literature at Zürich, Switzerland. The theory of "the art of loneliness" was stressed even more by Professor Staiger in a series of lectures on Goethe in the Fall of 1966 and Spring of 1967 attended by the present writer.

[101]Edfelt, Lyrik, pp. xx, xxi.

Richard Brigdman published "Emily Dickinson:
A Winter Poet in a Spring Land" in <u>Moderna
Språk</u>.[102] Brigdman first acknowledges the importance of Johnson's definitive editions of both
poems and letters. Brigdman finds that "her
[Dickinson's] correspondence possesses some of the
irritating features of her poetry--coyness, ellip-
tical obscurity, triviality."[103] But, on the
other hand, Brigdman continues, her letters contain "none of the pedestrian tedium of, let us
say, Melville's or Dreiser's. Indeed they are the
fabric of her poetry."[104] A good part of Brigdman's article is devoted to Dickinson's self-imposed limits: he argues that since her life was
certainly restricted, her images were bound to be
the same--domestic images, images of things she
knew well. Brigdman pays particular tribute to
her art of leaving out connectives, and to her
metaphors with "sustain traffic across the gaps."[105]
About a third of the article deals with Emily
Dickinson and death. He finds her puzzling over
death in the most realistic way and sees this pro-
cedure indeed as difficult for a New Englander who
was not supposed to relieve inner tensions by ex-
ternalizing grief. Finally, he sees death becom-
ing the lover, nothing new in the Christian tradition. "She profited by her seclusion to produce
a poetry of high thematic and technical interest
which so far in America has only been matched by

[102]Richard Brigdman, "Emily Dickinson: A
Winter Poet in a Spring Land," <u>Moderna Språk</u>, 56
(1962), 1-8. <u>Moderna Språk</u> is the scholarly publication of the Modern Language Teachers' Associ-
ation of Sweden.

[103]Brigdman, pp. 2-3. Cf. the similar remarks made by Österling, footnote 61.

[104]Brigdman, p. 3.

[105]Brigdman, p. 3.

Whitman," Brigdman concludes.[106]

1962 was a very special year in Swedish Dickinson criticism, for it was then that Brita Lindberg published her first article on Emily Dickinson, "The Theme of Death in Emily Dickinson's Poetry."[107] Later, Brita Lindberg became the acknowledged authority on Emily Dickinson in all of Scandinavia. In the above-mentioned article, Lindberg calls Dickinson's interest in death "[an] almost abnormal concern with the facts of dying."[108] The fact that such a large number of Dickinson's poems deal with death, Lindberg explains by Dickinson's having "attempted a sublimation of grief and an annihilation of her sense of loss."[109]

In discussing Dickinson's imagery, Lindberg maintains that "the techniques of familiarization, bringing abstractions and concepts which the human mind finds it difficult to visualize or grasp into the circle of our daily activities, is with Emily Dickinson so common that it must be regarded as a conscious stylistic trait."[110] In this way, even immortality is something that can be rendered in everyday terms. Even in the few poems where Emily Dickinson experiences horror of death, this same horror is mixed with a feeling of exhiliration. For her own fate, she seemingly has no fear, Lindberg states at the end of her article.

In 1965, Brita Lindberg turned to the tantaliz-

[106]Brigdman, p. 8.

[107]Brita Lindberg, "The Theme of Death in Emily Dickinson's Poetry," Studia Neophilologica, 37 (1965), 327-59. Subsequent references to this article will be cited as "Death."

[108]Lindberg, "Death," p. 270.

[109]Lindberg, "Death," p. 273.

[110]Lindberg, "Death," p. 276.

ing problem of Emily Dickinson's punctuation.[111]
Assuming that punctuation is indeed part of a
writer's style, even personality, she takes on the
task of proving her point. Cautiously, she states
in the introduction that she will not "propose a
radically new and final interpretation."[112] Instead, she wants to clarify some points, and to
rule out some interpretations that she considers
incorrect. The article has four divisions, apart
from the brief above-mentioned introduction and the
equally brief conclusion. The first division is
called "The Problem Defined" and it briefly out-
lines what particular problem awaits the Dickinson scholar regarding her punctuation: the enormous number of punctuation idiosyncrasies on the
part of the poet together with the fact that the
manuscripts themselves are of little help in that
they are open to various interpretations. The
second division, "Punctuation Marks in Print:
Theory and Practice," gives an over-view of what
some critics have said regarding the best handling of this punctuation. Lindberg concludes that
they mostly have suggested normalizing the punctuation (as in the case of, for instance, Anderson
and Johnson, although, Lindberg remarks, the latter did not follow his own recommendation). In
"The Elocutionary Theory," Lindberg judges this
theory "a shaky . . . hypothesis" quite unlikely
in the case of a poet who did not seek public acceptance. In the latest section, "Nineteenth-
century Theory and Practice," Lindberg remarks
that Dickinson was familiar with the dash as a
punctuation mark from childhood on. At first,
Dickinson must have used it unconsciously; later
on, it was used to give a conscious, artistic form.

[111]Brita Lindberg, "Emily Dickinson's Punctuation," Studia Neophilologica, 37 (1965), 327-59.
Subsequent references to this article will be
cited as "Punctuation."

[112]Lindberg, "Punctuation," p. 328.

The real significance of the dash, however, remains "hers alone."[113]

Erik Frykman in 1966 published "Sångens blixt-nedslag" ["The Lightning of Singing"].[114] As so often is the case, this article starts out as a brief review, this time of Albert J. Gelpi's book, Emily Dickinson: The Mind of the Poet (Cambridge, Mass.: Harvard University Press, 1965), but soon Frykman is giving his own opinions of Dickinson's poetry. He, like some other Swedes before him, sees Dickinson's isolation as voluntary and delib-erately decided upon: ". . . she was afraid of losing herself in living together with anyone else."[115] Frykman stresses Dickinson's ability to see "perspectives," not only the immediate moment; his proof is the fact that so many of her poems consider "eternally valid truths."

Roughly one year before his death, Erik Linde-gren in 1967 wrote two poems dedicated to Emily Dickinson.[116] He called them "Parafras" ["Para-phrase"] and "Gravskiss" ["Sketch of a Grave"]. Lindegren apparently has kept in mind that 4- and 3- beat lines were favorites of Dickinson. Both poems are structured the same way: all lines, ex-cept one, are 4-beat lines. The two poems are published under the title of "Två dikter för

[113]Lindberg, "Punctuation," p. 352.

[114]Erik Frykman, "Sångens blixtnedslag," Göteborgs Handels-och Sjöfartstidning, March 17, 1966, p. 3. Erik Frykman is professor of English at the University of Göteborg [Gothenburg]. Sub-sequent references to this article will be cited as "Blixtnedslaget."

[115]Frykman, "Blixtnedslaget," p. 3.

[116]Erik Lindegren, "Två dikter för speldosa till Emily Dickinsons ära: Parafras och Grav-skiss," Göteborgs Handels-och Sjöfartstidning, March 9, 1967, p. 3.

39

speldosa till Emily Dickinsons ära" ["Two Poems for a Music Box: Homage to Emily Dickinson"]. "Parafras" is a two-stanza poem, each stanza containing four lines. The theme deals with the problem of self-identification; not knowing oneself matters less, though, as long as one has "a blue parasol." The Dickinson poem that comes to mind is "In lands I never saw--they say" (called "Alper" ["The Alps"] in the 1949 Edfelt translation). The second poem, "Gravskiss," deals with a mouse which, in the end, turns out to be the only treasure of the poet. I was afraid of my house, muses the poet, because there was a mouse; yet, I slept as if the mouse were my one and only treasure. The poems both show a remarkable insight into the elusive poetic quality that was Emily Dickinson's.

Also, in 1967, Corinna [signature of Greta Bolin] published a short article, "Om sommaren sköna" ["In Summers So Sweet"] in Svenska Dagbladet.[117] Greta Bolin gives a nostalgic picture of how she "happened upon" Emily Dickinson in her bookcase while actually looking for something else. She tells the reader how the fascination she feels now is more than comparable to what she felt years ago: Dickinson's "syntactical revolution" and "passionate imagination" still hold the same spell. She sang of loneliness, Bolin remarks, much in the same way as Edith Södergran.[118] Both, she finds, write about the basic problems of love and death, immortality and eternity.

In Dickinson criticism originating in Sweden, the year 1968 so far remains the most important one. Following her articles on Emily Dickinson discussed above, Brita Lindberg-Seyersted published a comprehensive, in-depth book on Emily Dickin-

[117]Greta Bolin, "Om sommaren sköna," Svenska Dagbladet, August 10, 1967, p. 12.

[118]Cf. footnote 68.

son; the book itself grew out of Lindberg's doctoral dissertation.[119] In the book, Lindberg does
not approach literary interpretations in a traditional manner; her purpose has been two-fold, she
states in the preface. First, she wanted to ex-
plore Dickinson's poetic language. Second, she
wanted to use modern linguistics in an analysis of
the poet's words. Thomas H. Johnson found "the
work impressive," judging the "scholarship impeccable, wide-ranging, and up-to-date."[120] The work
certainly is learned, even esoteric, blending
solid insight into modern linguistics with equally
solid knowledge of more traditional literary interpretation.

After more than two years, Erik Frykman re-
turned with "Emily Dickinson och språket" ["Emily
Dickinson and the Language"].[121] In this case,
the major part is a review of Lindberg's work,
which he calls a "stylistic study." On the whole,
Frykman is positive in his evaluation of the study;
however, he is critical of the range of purposes
involved, such as "distinguishing between the successful and the less successful" in Dickinson's
poetry. Frykman discusses, among other things,
Dickinson's vocabulary, noting that genuine in-
novations seldom occur in her poetry. He observes

[119]Brita Lindberg-Seyersted, The Voice of the
Poet: Aspects of Style in the Poetry of Emily
Dickinson (Cambridge, Mass.: Harvard University
Press, 1968). Brita Lindberg-Seyersted now teaches
American literature at the University of Oslo,
Norway. Since the book was originally written in
English and is available from Harvard University
Press, the review of Lindberg's book will not be
as extensive as that of other material.

[120]Johnson, quoted on the cover of Lindberg's
book.

[121]Erik Frykman, "Emily Dickinson och språket," Svenska Dagbladet, May 31, 1968, p. 5.

41

that she does combine ordinary adjectives with
less ordinary noun endings, and that she generally
plays with word classes in an unorthodox way.
Frykman gives no examples of Dickinson's playing
with word classes. He does say, however, that he
considers Milton the most probable influence in
sharp contrast to Lindberg who stresses the influence of Shakespeare.

In the same month, Brita Lindberg published
some brief remarks on the poem "Superfluous were
the Sun."[122] She offers the suggestion that the
parting scene of that poem does not deal with the
abandonment of a lover by the beloved one. Instead, she sees the scene as referring to actual
physical death. Lindberg gives several reasons
for this reading. She attempts to explain the
poem largely in linguistic terms. Also, she observes that parting in Dickinson more often refers
to literal parting due to death than to any other
kind of parting.

Between 1968 and 1972, there is a hiatus in
Dickinson criticism in Sweden. The fact that
nothing was published in four years apparently did
not mean that Emily Dickinson had ceased to interest scholars, or that she did not have a faithful
general reading public. Her popularity is testified to by a translation competition that Västmanlands Läns Tidning sponsored in 1972.[123] The interest in the competition was so great and the
quality of contributions so excellent, says the

[122]Brita Lindberg, "Further Notes on a Poem
by Emily Dickinson," Notes and Queries, 213 (May
1968), 179-80.

[123][Anders Yngve Pers], "Färdigdiktat om
Emily Dickinson" ["Enough Dickinson Poetry"],
Västmanlands Läns Tidning, February 16, 1972,
p. 12. The anonymous writer is Anders Yngve Pers,
owner and editor-in-chief of VLT at the time and
member of the prestigious Pers newspaper dynasty.

anonymous writer, that no first prize could be awarded. Instead, every contributor was to get a letter expressing the appreciation of the newspaper.

Six months later, Ruth Halldén wrote a long article for Dagens Nyheter, "Levande dikt ur en frusen kvinna" ["Live Poetry out of a Frozen Woman"].[124] Halldén's frame of reference is the psychiatrist John Cody and his Freudian reading of Emily Dickinson (John Cody, After Great Pain: The Inner Life of Emily Dickinson, Cambridge, Mass.: The Belknap Press of Harvard University Press, 1971). According to Halldén, certainly Dickinson was pathologically afraid of darkness as well as of people. More than anything else, her dreamed-up lovers reveal her "as the psychiatric case she was." It is so common, Halldén agrees with Cody, that sexually unfulfilled women fantasize about demanding lovers that this aberration rightly has a name of its own--Clerambault's syndrome. Her mother, apparently supplying her children with little love, together with "the senseless Puritanism of New England," was the prime factor in making Emily psychotic, argues Halldén. Her poetry is typical of a certain stage of the dissolution of a person: infantile emotional reactions combined with intellectual insights. She is geared to interpreting "elusive psychological processes" which, later on, Freud would do in a more single-minded and purposeful way. She "moves around in her subconscious as the rest of us do in the conscious world," Halldén says in her concluding remarks.[125]

Using Halldén's article as a starting-point, Kerstin Strandberg, only two weeks later, wrote a somewhat unusual article on Emily Dickinson for

[124]Ruth Halldén, "Levande dikt ur en frusen kvinna," Dagens Nyheter, August 14, 1972, p. 4.

[125]Halldén, p. 4.

43

Dagens Nyheter, this one untitled.[126] The article
discusses the possible sociological background for
sexual mores of past centuries and even of the
twentieth century. Emily Dickinson is used as an
example of what happens to the sexually unfulfilled individual, mostly female, herself only a victim of past caprices of religion, even of economy.
"To continue to work for sexual liberation is pro-
gressive," Strandberg concludes her article.[127]

Only three days after Strandberg, Ann-Marie
Lund gave her passionate support of Emily Dickinson in an article for Dagens Nyheter, "Skulle
Emily ha gift sig med pastorsadjunkten?" ["Should
Emily Have Married the Reverend?"].[128] After
reading "the article on the culture page of August
14,"[129] there are many questions that "ignorant
but dedicated Dickinson admirers" must ask themselves, Lund writes.[130] We have now been told,
Lund continues, that we must look at Emily Dickinson "as the psychiatric case she was." But would
anybody view, Lund questions, Strindberg "as the
psychiatric case he was," rather than as an erup-
tive and multi-faceted genius? Under the sub-
title of "Kan man bortse från dikterna?" ["Can
One Disregard the Poetry?"], Lund argues that in
discussing an individual's mental life one should

[126]Kerstin Strandberg, "Motroten," Dagens
Nyheter, August 28, 1972, p. 5. Although the
article itself is untitled, it appears under a
particular, regularly used title, "Motroten," a
Swedish anagram.

[127]Strandberg, p. 5.

[128]Ann-Marie Lund, "Skulle Emily ha gift sig
med pastorsadjunkten?", Dagens Nyheter, August 31,
1972, p. 4.

[129]I.e., Halldén's article.

[130]Lund, p. 4.

44

consider the products and outcome of this mental
life, in this case the poems. For the ordinary
reader, these poems not only express ecstasy and
intellectual insight, but they also "bubble with"
the kind of spirituality and high-spirited playfulness that one finds only in rare geniuses.

To deal with the problem of dying is a natural human concern, Lund maintains in the part of
the article sub-titled "Dödens problem otidsen-
ligt?" ["Is the Problem of Death Outdated?"].[131]
In "Den sexuella försakelsen" ["The Sexual Sacrifice"], Lund discusses the above-mentioned Cler-
ambault's syndrome.[132] To "the ordinary reader,"
Lund writes, Emily's love poetry certainly seems
to deal with tangible and natural experiences,
i.e., natural in her milieu and time. In "Funk-
tionellt att hon isolerade sig" ["Her Isolation
Was Functional"], Lund asks: "An explosion of
genius that happened to be born in a little Puritan town in New England in the middle of the nineteenth century--what was Emily supposed to do?
Marry the Reverend?"[133] Lund fittingly finishes
her article by quoting the first stanza of "Much
Madness is divinest Sense."

In 1974, Lennart Breitholtz edited the last
part of Litteraturens klassiker i urval och översättning [Selected and Translated Literary

[131]Many critics share Lund's opinion that it
is natural for anyone to be concerned about death,
perhaps particularly for someone in Emily Dickinson's time and milieu where death could often be
observed at close quarters. The fullest critical
discussion of how the problem of dying affected
Emily Dickinson was made by Thomas W. Ford in
Heaven Beguiles the Tired: Death in the Poetry of
Emily Dickinson (University, Ala.: University of
Alabama Press, 1966).

[132]Halldén's article.

[133]Lund, p. 4.

Classics].[134] Dr. Breitholtz selected eight poems
by Emily Dickinson, a larger number than for any
other English-speaking poet (Whitman has seven,
Poe three, and Emily Brontë one, in comparison).
In his preface, Dr. Breitholtz states that the only
purpose of the translator (in the case of the
English poetry, Dr. Lars Lindvall) has been to
facilitate the understanding of the poems; thus,
the translation is given in prose at the bottom of
each page.

Strictly speaking, this book from 1974 marks
the end of the Dickinson criticism from the Swedish mainland as of 1977. Back in the 1930's,
Encyclopaedia Britannica did not mention Emily
Dickinson and the same was true for Nordisk Familjebok in the early 1920's.[135] In 1953, Svensk
Uppslagsbok [The Swedish Reference Book] had almost one full page dedicated to Emily Dickinson.[136]
It contains, predictably, a fairly large amount of
biographical material as well as a small list of
selected critics.[137] Most of the material, however, deals with the themes and language of Dickinson's poetry, seeing "life and love, nature and

[134]Lennart Breitholtz, ed., Litteraturens
klassiker i urval och översättning (Stockholm:
Almqvist och Wiksell, 1974), XVIII, 104-10. The
Dickinson poems are: "Success is counted sweetest";
"The Soul selects her own Society"; "A Bird came
down the Walk"; "Much Madness is divinest Sense";
"The Heart asks Pleasure--first"; "Because I could
not stop for Death"; "After a hundred years"; and
"My life closed twice before its close."

[135]Cf. footnote 12 and the first paragraph of
this chapter.

[136]Svensk Uppslagsbok (Malmö: Förlagshuset
Norden A. B., 1955), VII, 354-55.

[137]Among the critics mentioned are Bianchi,
Taggard, Whicher, Abenius, and Bingham, spanning
the years between 1924 and 1945.

eternity" as her main themes and describing her
language as independent of traditional metrics and
syntax.

There is nothing surprising, of course, in
the fact that The World Book Encyclopedia, one of
the American reference books that one would find
in almost every Swedish library and mentioned here
for that very reason, considers Emily Dickinson
"one of the most important woman poets of the
United States" as well as "one of the chief in-
fluences on present-day poetry."[138] Bonniers
Lexicon, published by the biggest publishing house
in Scandinavia, in 1962 describes her poetry as
altogether a personal confession, ranging from
shy intimateness to an open expression of strong
feelings, and as having "condensed, simple imagery" and "strong linguistic authority."[139] The
bibliographical material is brief: only three
full-length books are mentioned, namely the
Edfelt-Blomberg translations and the two books entitled Emily Dickinson by Ellen Löfmarck and Richard Chase, respectively.

Lilla Uppslagsboken [The Little Reference
Book] deserves its name; its entries are indeed
brief.[140] Nevertheless, the Emily Dickinson entry
contains various kinds of information: biographical,
an appreciative thematic and linguistic evaluation
of her poetry, and also two bibliographical references, namely Johnson's biography and Abenius'
Kontakter.[141]

[138]The World Book Encyclopedia (Chicago: Field
Enterprises Educational Corporation, 1960), IV, 156.

[139]Uno Dalén et al., eds., Bonniers Lexicon
(Stockholm: AB Nordiska Uppslagsböcker, 1962), p. 972.

[140]Lilla Uppslagsboken (Malmö: Förlagshuset
Norden AB, 1965), II, 899.

[141]Cf. footnote 23.

47

In *Focus Uppslagsbok* [Focus Reference Book], one can read that Emily Dickinson is "one of America's foremost poets comparable to Whitman in her power of expression."[142] Blomberg, Edfelt, and Löfmarck are mentioned in the field of translation.

Finally, the briefest entry of all is to be found in *Norstedts Uppslagsbok* [Norstedt's Reference Book]. It calls Emily Dickinson one of the finest American poets by virtue of her "linguistic ability and originality."[143]

The content of even a representative number of reference works may seem irrelevant to the literary reputation of a writer. However, it is one thing to be "discovered," even lionized, by a scholar or *Schöngeist*[144] in a given country. "The ordinary reader," in Ann-Marie Lund's words, is quite another thing. The question of whether an artist has really penetrated the consciousness of a nation is to be solved only in considering the ordinary, albeit well-educated, reader. Dickinson's appearance in reference works suggests that the poet is firmly established in Sweden.

Sweden, moreover, does not consist of only the geographical mainland of Sweden. Culturally, some seven percent of Finland is still part of Sweden in the sense that this part of the population is bilingual.[145] In intellectual circles, no

[142]*Focus Uppslagsbok* (Stockholm: Almqvist och Wiksell Förlag AB, 1970), II, 611.

[143]*Norstedts Uppslagsbok* (Stockholm: P. A. Norstedt och Söners Förlag, 1973), p. 265.

[144]German word used as a loan-word in all of Europe designating an esthete inclined toward the more esoteric aspects of all of the fine arts.

[145]Finland, for a very long time, was a Swedish colony. Although this part of Swedish-Finnish

great distinction has ever been made between riks-
svenskar and finlandssvenskar.[146]

The first to translate Emily Dickinson in
Swedish-speaking Finland was Lars von Haartman.[147]
In Nya Argus, one of the best literary magazines
in Finland, he translated four poems.[148] One has
to be grateful that a poet of Haartman's stature
took on this task. A less known translator but a
well-known literary critic, Alarik Roos, published
the article "Överraskningarnas skaldinna" ["The

---

history lies several hundred years back, many ties,
the most important one being the language, are
still strong. Swedish was once number one of the
two official languages; nowadays, of course, it is
number two, after Finnish.

[146]Rikssvenskar means Swedes of the Kingdom;
finlandssvenskar means Swedes from the Republic of
Finland.

[147]Lars von Haartman, poet, translator, and
professor of Zoology at the University of Helsingfors [Helsinki]. Among his literary publications
are the following poetry collections: Reseskild-
ring [Travelogue] (Helsingfors: Holger Schildts
Förlag, 1960); Svarta Segel [Black Sails] (Helsingfors: Holger Schildts Förlag, 1979); Vinterljus
[Winter Light] (Helsingfors: Holger Schildts Förlag, 1977).

[148]Lars von Haartman, "Fyra dikter av Emily
Dickinson" ["Four Poems by Emily Dickinson"], Nya
Argus, 19 (1961), 289. The four poems translated
are: "Nature rarer uses Yellow"; "We learn in the
Retreating"; "To fight aloud, is very brave"; and
"Not knowing when the Dawn will come." At this
time, Haartman had been translating Dickinson for
years, more for his own pleasure than with a view
toward publication--perhaps like his favorite poet,
Emily Dickinson. (Letter received from Lars von
Haartman, 7 September 1977).

Poetess of Surprises"].[149]   He begins with his own
translation of "There's a certain Slant of light."
Roos uses the poem as an example of how different-
ly critics have interpreted Dickinson's poetry;
this particular poem can be seen as dealing with
grief, with heavenly light, with death, and many
other themes. It is one of Dickinson's special
accomplishments, Roos maintains, to be able to
suggest both movement and stillness seemingly at
the same time by a kind of metamorphosis. She is
the poetess of surprises, Roos quotes Helen af
Enehjelm who, in 1946, said that in the English-
speaking world very few had understood Emily Dick-
inson--but that the Swedes had interpreted her
correctly. This lack of understanding, Roos hastens to add, has changed in the last few decades.
Many critics still, however, do not seem to understand her "playing with words and syntax." Few
have been artistically conscious to the same degree, Roos writes. Her imagery is blinding like
lightning--one can hardly expect her to be "pro-
fessorial." In support of his own view that one
"does not have to know everything" about a poet's
reasons, ways, and methods to appreciate the poetry properly, Roos cites Emil Staiger.[150]   In his
great work on Goethe, Staiger argues, according to
Roos, that there comes a point where the biograph-
er, or critic, has to hold back, discreetly, because of the scarcity of the material or, perhaps,
of the intimate nature of the problem. Instead,
one must simply enjoy the poetry that is actually
there, as a wealth of surprises.

   In 1968, Lars von Haartman twice published
Dickinson translations. In the first instance,
there are five translations ("The thought beneath
so slight a film"; "Safe in their Alabaster

[149]Alarik Roos, "Överraskningarnas skaldinna,"
Hufvudstadsbladet, December 9, 1967, p. 7.

[150]Cf. footnote 100.

Chambers"; "Lay this Laurel on the One"; "Doom is the House without the Door"; and "Oh Sumptuous moment").[151] The other translation, also in Nya Argus, is of "There's a certain Slant of light.[152]

Alarik Roos in 1969 published "Poesin som struktur" ["Poetry as Structure"].[153] The title refers to Brita Lindberg's book which he reviews in part of the article. But Roos concentrates on an old problem: is poetry structure? If it is, is it only that, or does it perhaps have also other ingredients? He argues that certainly in poetry, structure must be inseparable from content, or may indeed be content, as Lindberg's book suggests.

In 1970, Lars von Haartman published two translated poems, one of Dickinson and one of Robert Bly.[154] It is worthwhile keeping in mind that as versatile a poet and translator as Haartman does not only concentrate on Dickinson. It is perhaps also fitting to finish the references to Dickinson translations within the Swedish-speaking culture with Haartman who, at this time [1977], seems to be the only one continuing to translate Dickinson.[155]

[151] Lars von Haartman, "Dikter av Emily Dickinson" ["Poems by Emily Dickinson"], Nya Argus, 7 (1968), 96.

[152] Lars von Haartman, "There's a certain Slant of light," Nya Argus, 19 (1968), 293.

[153] Alarik Roos, "Poesin som struktur," Hufvudstadsbladet, October 3, 1969, p. 9.

[154] Lars von Haartman, "Amerikanska dikter" ["American Poems"], Nya Argus, 10-11 (1970), 168.

[155] Erik Blomberg is dead. The perhaps best Swedish-speaking translator, Lars von Haartman, is planning to publish a collection of American poetry translated into Swedish. Most of the poems will be

51

Vivi-Ann Hakalax wrote "USA-lyriker erkänd efter sin död: Arvet efter Emily Dickinson--1700 opublicerade dikter" ["U.S. Poet Acclaimed after Her Death: The Legacy of Emily Dickinson--1700 Unpublished Poems"] in Hufvudstadsbladet.[156] She observes that Dickinson's world is one of "paradoxes, metaphors, and aphorisms." Reading her poetry is an intense emotional experience and it is remarkable how the imagery of such brief poems can convey so much of the joy and grief of living. With great humility, she continues, Dickinson admits her lack of ability to solve the riddles of life and death; in life, this fact made her isolate herself, and in poetry, it led her to look for the most economic expression.[157] Emily regarded her own intensity as a handicap, Hakalax continues; yet, her intensity goes hand in hand with her so-called intuition, i.e., her amazing insight into people. When an individual feels the pressures of life too intensely, he may well lose some of his mental balance and Emily Dickinson's poetry is proof of just that. However, we, as readers, need not be concerned about her lack of adjustment to life; instead, we should concen-

---

by Emily Dickinson, but he also intends to include Pound, Bly, Merwin, and others. (Letter received from Lars von Haartman, 6 September 1977). A first-rate artist, in addition to his other accomplishments, Haartman has himself illustrated most of his Dickinson translations, whereas Blomberg-Edfelt used the well-known artist Yngve Berg (see footnote 36).

[156]Vivi-Ann Hakalax, "USA-lyriker erkänd efter sin död: Arvet efter Emily Dickinson--1700 opublicerade dikter," Hufvudstadsbladet, September 8, 1973, p. Lördagsextra 3.

[157]Cf. Löfmarck in "Emily, ensamheten och Gud," footnote 94. Löfmarck argues that "economy" in living and "economy" in writing are functions

trate on the quality of Dickinson's artistry,
Hakalax concludes her article. Emily Dickinson
sings to conquer the horror of living while
stretching toward a cosmic vision.

Five M. A. theses on Emily Dickinson were
written at the University of Helsinki between 1965
and 1977. One, Marja Monto's "Religious Metaphors
and the Theme of Religiosity in the Poetry of
Emily Dickinson," will be summarized here.[158]
Monto, following the lead of most critics, first
gives a long biographical background, including
"the religious development" (chapter II) as it can
be seen in Dickinson's spiritual crises and the
ensuing religious skepticism. Most of the thesis
deals with different metaphors, such as the ones
used for God or for immortality. Monto writes
that Dickinson mostly regards the latter as a

---

of the same background.

[158]Marja Monto, "Religious Metaphors and the
Theme of Religiosity in the Poetry of Emily Dickinson," M. A. Thesis University of Helsingfors [Hel-
sinki], 1977. For copyright reasons, the other
four M. A. theses from the University of Helsingfors can be only briefly mentioned. Raili Partan-
en wrote "A Study of Emily Dickinson's Adjectives,"
1965; Partanen attempts to define the ways adjectives are used with regard to nature, objects, the
mind and soul, etc. Kirsikka Vesa wrote "Verbal
Repetition in the Poems of Emily Dickinson," 1967,
a purely linguistic study. Pirkko Sihto's thesis
is entitled "Personifikaatio Emily Dickinsonin
Runoudessa Ja Kirjeissa" ["Personification in the
Poetry and the Letters of Emily Dickinson"], n.d.
This thesis covers linguistic aspects of personification as well as the whole range of tangible
and intangible nouns being personified. Finally,
Marja-Leena Tolonen discussed "The Theme of Loneliness in Emily Dickinson's Poetry," 1975. The
thesis deals with well-known aspects of Dickinson's

"conscious state of man after death" and therefore
uses tangible things as metaphors.[159] Monto, in
her final chapter, sees Dickinson's mind as a center of contradictory feelings and convictions.
She did not "believe" in her Puritan surroundings
and upbringing; yet, she could not free herself.
It is Monto's opinion that writing poetry was the
only way for Dickinson to resolve the conflict.
One might comment that, in all probability, every
artistic product, whether literary, musical, or
visual, contains exactly those seeds: it is the
explosion and, as such, the resolution of otherwise unbearable problems.

Summary of Swedish and Swedish-Finnish Criticism
of Emily Dickinson

It took a relatively long time for Emily
Dickinson's poetry to gain general acceptance in
Sweden. The reasons for this late recognition
range from the fact that the Swedes were already
used to highly unconventional poetry, to the fact
that political viewpoints fostered a certain cultural wariness regarding the United States--a
wariness that did not abate until the early 1930's.
Only twice was Emily Dickinson mentioned in the
Swedish press of the thirties. In 1934, Margit
Abenius wrote a highly appreciative article on
Dickinson (see footnote 3). Abenius emphasized
the quality of Dickinson's death poetry which she
ranks among the best of its kind in the world.
Not surprisingly, Erik Blomberg, himself a first-
rate poet, was the other critic to deal with Dickinson in the thirties. He chose the same literary
magazine as Abenius did, the avante-garde Bonniers
Litterära Magasin, to publish his translations of

---

poetry: alienation, death, immortality, beauty and
truth, and finally, different kinds of love.

[159]Monto, p. 26.

three Dickinson poems (see footnote 9).

The forties saw thirteen published items dealing with Dickinson, ranging from five publication previews to one full-length book of translations. Four of the publications were articles. Two items were chapters of full-length books and still another one was a translation of two Dickinson poems.

Of the six articles (and chapters), those of Edfelt, Abenius, Lindegren, Lindqvist, and Löfmarck (in chronological order) are highly appreciative. Edfelt suggests that Dickinson is superior to all other American poets and pays particular tribute to her innovative language and to the quality of her love poetry (see footnote 10). Abenius' chapter is a reprint of her 1934 article; she, too, considers Dickinson the best American poet and is particularly appreciative of the death poetry (see footnote 23). Lindegren pays tribute to "the independent soul" of Dickinson; two decades later he was to dedicate two poems to her (see footnote 25). Lindqvist, in her article, treats the themes of Dickinson and comments on the relationship between Dickinson's personal life and her poetry: the poet could treat the whole spectrum of human emotions despite her own restricted experiences (see footnote 30). Löfmarck, in her first article on Dickinson, out of many to come, attempts a balanced evaluation of Dickinson, but comes near the Edfelt appreciation in calling Dickinson's poetry "the greatest poetic treasure of America" (see footnotes 35 and 39). Artur Lundkvist alone differs from the above-mentioned critics. In his chapter on, among others, Dickinson, he admits to being impressed by her; yet, he does not consider her first-rate. His criticism is particularly directed toward the form of her poetry (see footnote 17).

Edfelt is the last one, as well as the first, to publish on Dickinson in the forties. Fittingly, it is a full-length collection of poetry that

he publishes in 1949 in collaboration with Erik
Blomberg (see footnote 36). In addition, he had
translated two poems in 1944 (see footnote 22).
With the 1949 book, Emily Dickinson is definitely
established in Sweden.

Löfmarck's book, <u>Emily Dickinson</u>, marks the
beginning of a decade that saw a rush of Dickinson
criticism (see footnote 47). Twenty-three items
were published; of these, the first is Löfmarck's
book, eighteen are articles, and four are publication previews. In 1950 alone, eleven articles
were published together with two publication previews, apart from Löfmarck's book. It is now obvious that Dickinson is well established: Löfmarck's book gives both a thematic and linguistic
analysis of the poet, as well as translations of a
great number of poems. Of the eleven articles of
1950, only one is unfavorable and as such reminiscent of the Lundkvist essay of 1942. The article
is Carlson's "Ett amerikanskt diktaröde."[160] Of
the other critics of 1950, Jaensson, Liedgren (the
theologian), and Fehrman concentrate on Dickinson's theme of death or eternity (see footnotes
51, 56, and 67). Ridderstad, Österling, Lindqvist,
Levander, and Landquist concentrate on form or
language (see footnotes 55, 58, 61, 64, 69 and 77).
Of these five critics, Lagercrantz' article is
different in that he attempts to summarize the
Dickinson scholarship in Sweden at this point in
time (see footnote 74).

Of the remaining 1950 articles, two dealt
with Dickinson's letters. Löfmarck bases her discussion on Mabel Loomis Todd's 1951 edition of
letters judging the quality of the letters comparable to that of the poetry (see footnote 78).
Still, Löfmarck argues, Dickinson is first of all

[160]See footnote 71. Whether the fact that both
Lundkvist and Carlson were notably left-oriented is
the common denominator operating in their judgments
of Emily Dickinson's poetry, is a question one can
only speculate on.

a poet. Johannes Edfelt deals with Dickinson's
letters to the Hollands (see footnote 81). He is
more appreciative of Dickinson's prose than Löfmarck and sees exactly the same qualities in both
letters and poetry.

Both Ellen Löfmarck and Birger Christoffersson discuss Rebecca Patterson's suggestion of lesbianism in their respective articles, "Gåtan Emily
Dickinson" and "Emily Dickinsons hemlighet" (see
footnotes 83 and 87, respectively). Löfmarck
finds some merit in Patterson's book while Christoffersson finds it totally convincing. Christoffersson, in "Emily Dickinsons teknik," praises
Dickinson's linguistic skills (see footnote 86).
Löfmarck added another article to her previous
ones, this one mainly to pay tribute to Thomas
Johnson's contribution to Dickinson scholarship
(see footnote 89). Finally, in this decade, Mats
Molander argues that Dickinson's self-imposed isolation is the core of her poetry (see footnote 91).

Despite the fact that only thirteen items were
published on Emily Dickinson in the sixties, the
decade so far remains the most important one in
Swedish Dickinson criticism. No questions are
raised any more as to the quality of Dickinson's
poetry, and the critics, with two exceptions (Ekman and Bolin), are well-established experts in
literary criticism. All of Brita Lindberg-Seyersted's publications mentioned here fall within this
decade. Her first two publications were articles
analyzing, respectively, death as a major theme in
Dickinson's poetry and the problem of Dickinson's
punctuation (see footnotes 107 and 111, respectively). The same two topics are dealt with in Lindberg's major publication, The Voice of the Poet:
Aspects of Style in the Poetry of Emily Dickinson
(see footnote 119). Lindberg's main concern has
been stylistic problems as the title indicates.
Later in the decade, Lindberg published a brief
article regarding the reading of one poem (see
footnote 122). Of particular interest is the fact
that a translation of "I died for Beauty" appeared

in a magazine geared to the general public, a fact
which might be considered the ultimate tribute to
the poet (see footnotes 96 and 97). Similar tributes are paid by Johannes Edfelt who includes
three Dickinson poems in a world-wide poetry selection (see footnote 98); and by Erik Lindegren--
both members of The Eighteen--who, in 1967, dedicated two poems to Dickinson (see footnote 116).
Erik Frykman, professor of American literature,
published two articles on Dickinson (see footnotes
114 and 121); the same is true for Ellen Löfmarck
(see footnotes 93 and 94).

Of the five items published so far [1977] in
the seventies, the first one again testifies to
the popularity Emily Dickinson enjoyed with the
general public. This item is the translation competition sponsored by Västmanlands Läns Tidning,
in 1972 (see footnote 123). Then three scholarly
articles followed in 1972. Ruth Halldén discussed
the love poetry in the light of Dickinson's alleged
sexual frustration (see footnote 124). Kerstin
Strandberg, in the same vein, saw in Dickinson the
perfect example of a sexually suppressed woman
(see footnote 126). Ann-Marie Lund, in sharp dis-
agreement with Halldén, saw Dickinson's love poetry as perfectly normal and "ordinary" (see footnote 128). Finally, Lennart Breitholtz included
eight Dickinson poems in what he calls "literary
classics" (see footnote 134). The additional fact
that Swedish reference books since 1953 devote
substantial space to Dickinson underscores her
standing as a poet.

At last, in Swedish-speaking Finland, several
translations and three articles appeared between
1961-1977, in addition to five M. A. theses. The
major name here is Lars von Haartman, who is author of almost all the translations (see footnotes
148, 151, 152, and 154). Alarik Roos is the author of two highly appreciative articles (see footnotes 149 and 153), and Vivi-Ann Hakalax of one
(see footnote 156).

This over-view of Dickinson criticism and

translations within the Swedish-speaking area of
Europe reflects a pattern of increasing appreciation as the years pass. What the two countries
culturally closest to Sweden, Norway and Denmark,
have contributed to the general picture of Dickinson in Europe will be considered in the next
chapter.

III. Norway and Denmark

     Norway and Denmark closely resemble Sweden in
literary climate. This resemblance is not surprising since Norway was part of the Kingdom of Sweden
for almost 100 years, the alliance ending in 1905.
Also, southernmost Sweden was part of the Kingdom
of Denmark for quite some time.[1] Despite the distinctly different languages of the three countries,
the common denominators outweigh the differences.

     Inger Hagerup first introduced Emily Dickin-
son to the Norwegian public.[2] Again as before in
Sweden, a first-rate poet initially realized the
quality of Dickinson's poetry. In an article of
1943, Hagerup calls Dickinson "a poet of unusual
dimensions . . . by many considered America's
greatest together with Walt Whitman."[3] Dickinson's
poetry is the kind that lends itself to being re-
explored, Hagerup maintains; it is timeless and
therefore always modern. Dickinson writes about

     [1]The alliance functioned intermittently from
the Middle Ages and even into modern times. A lay-
man cannot accurately date the span of the relationship because of the legal complexity in defining citizenship and proprietary rights.

     [2]Inger Hagerup, "Emily Dickinson: En kvinne-
lig lyriker" ["Emily Dickinson: A Woman Poet"],
Urd, 4 (January 23, 1943), 53-54. Hagerup has
published close to ten collections of poetry, including many translated poems, and is also the author of three collections of children's verse,
plays, etc. Even her son, Helge Hagerup, who himself has five plays, poetry, prose, detective
stories, etc., to his credit, is most often referred
to as the son of his famous mother (Östgöta Correspondenten [Sweden], June 3, 1977, p. 6).

     [3]Hagerup, p. 53.

the core of living: of nature, love, and death.
The hymn-book rhythm is simple, not to say sometimes monotonous, but the reader tends to forget
the words as such, because of the importance of
the content. It is her message which remains.
"She is the Sappho of the nineteenth century,"
Hagerup continues without elaborating the point.

Hagerup, in her final remarks, considers
Dickinson's poetry the purest example of "l'art
pour l'art."[4] She ends the article by giving two
Dickinson poems in translation, one of them being
"Flukt" ["What if I say I· shall not wait!"] and
the other one "Död er den siste dialog" ["Death is
a Dialogue between"]. One year later, she published two translations in the Swedish Bonniers Litterära Magasin, one of them the same as in 1943,
"Död er den siste dialog," and the other one being
"For skjönnhet döde jag" ["I died for Beauty"].[5]

In 1949, Inger Hagerup published another
article on Emily Dickinson.[6] Emily Dickinson's
poetry is that of a "genius," Hagerup maintains.
"It is not easy for an admirer of Emily Dickinson
to evaluate her art unless one wants to dissect
perfect art," Hagerup continues, but Dickinson
herself dissects both her thoughts and feelings.[7]

[4]This statement seems to indicate that Hagerup regards Dickinson's form as perhaps superior to
her message. If this is the way to read the statement, it is contradictory to Hagerup's first remarks about Dickinson's "words" and "message."

[5]Inger Hagerup, "To dikt om döden" ["Two
Poems about Death"], Bonniers Litterära Magasin,
5 (1944), 399.

[6]Inger Hagerup, "Emily Dickinson," Vinduet,
[n.v.] (1949), pp. 419-24. Subsequent references
to this article will be cited as "ED."

[7]Hagerup, "ED," p. 422.

As artist, she belongs to the intellectual kind that fanatically searches for the precise expression. Behind the controlled form "lie an ocean of distress and dearly paid-for life experiences." It is this very mixture of control and panic that makes for "the tension that I, personally, have found in the production of no other poet," Hagerup continues.[8] Dickinson writes of death, love, and passion. Yet, it is time that is her constant preoccupation, Hagerup argues. Her blending of time and the timeless is as bold as if she were Einstein; probably her own very special view of time explains why she showed no particular interest in being recognized by her contemporaries. Instead, the fame of the future would do equally well, given her particular view of time. And, Hagerup concludes, she was right. Dickinson's poetry belongs to the future; the poems contain the very essence of immortality.

Hagerup adds four translated poems to her article, none of which had been translated by her before. They are "Hva er Paradis?" ["What is—'Paradise'"]; "Du sa en dag at jeg var 'stor'" ["You said I 'was Great'—one Day"]; "Alt har hun prøvd i livet" ["Whatever it is—she has tried it"]; and "Selv velger sjelen selskap for seg selv" ["The Soul selects her own Society"].

In 1957, Paal Brekke published _Amerikansk lyrikk: Et utvalg i norsk gjendiktning_ [American Poetry: A Selection of Norwegian Translations].[9] Brekke selected twelve poems by Emily Dickinson, more than by any other poet, including Whitman.[10]

[8]Hagerup, "ED," p. 423.

[9]Paal Brekke, _Amerikansk lyrikk: Et utvalg i norsk gjendiktning_ (Oslo: Aschehoug og Co., 1957), pp. 26-32, 119-22.

[10]The twelve poems translated are: "I never saw a Moor"; "A Bird came down the Walk"; "He ate and drank the precious Words"; "I taste a liquor never brewed"; "Surgeons must be very careful";

In his critical commentary, he calls her "the most important woman poet in the English language." It is no wonder, Brekke continues, that this century appreciates Dickinson more in every decade. For this we have to thank T. S. Eliot; following his essay on the Metaphysical poets published in 1921, the renewed interest in the masters of irony and paradox would naturally include Emily Dickinson. However, Brekke adds, it does happen that the particular format of her poetry strikes one as stereotyped and monotonous. What saves it, though, is the dramatic changes of tone, the boldness of the thought, and the novelty of her images. Brekke concludes that when it comes to "aphoristic virtuosity," Dickinson may be unequalled anywhere. In his last sentence, Brekke pays tribute to Inger Hagerup "who introduced her [Emily Dickinson] after the war with four translations and who has also dedicated one of her own finest poems to her."[11]

In 1960, Sigmund Skard published Under nye stjerner: Amerikansk lyrikk gjennom 300 år [Under New Stars: American Poetry through 300 Years].[12]

"Talk with prudence to a Beggar"; "Success is counted sweetest"; "Much Madness is divinest Sense"; "I'm Nobody! Who are you?"; "The Only News I know"; "My life closed twice before its close"; and "Will there really be a 'Morning'?."

[11]The "four translations" referred to must be the ones from 1949 (see footnote 6), but Hagerup, of course, also published two translations in 1943 (see footnote 2) as well as two in 1944 (see footnote 5). The poem dedicated to Emily Dickinson is "Meget spinkel. Meget liten." ["Very fragile. Very small."].

[12]Sigmund Skard, Under nye Stjerner: Amerikansk lyrikk gjennom 300 år (Oslo: Gyldendal Norsk Forlag, 1960), pp. 20-23, 92-107. Subsequent references to this book will be cited as Stjerner.

Skard translated a sizeable number of Dickinson poems and also wrote an introduction to them. Emily Dickinson, Skard writes, makes the narrow limits of Amherst burst by her own inner life and "terrifying honesty." Like Emerson and Whitman, she has a soul constantly questioning the world. But her doubts go deeper than do theirs, he maintains. Her mind lacks the respect for things that one might expect a mind of her century to show. She belongs in the twentieth century. She meets her problems head-on with no audience but herself. She sought an expression for herself, her identity, and her position in the cosmos, Skard continues.

Together with all this went an unusual sense of humor; the paradox was her natural mode of thinking. She can be flippant and gay, Skard reminds the reader, despite the fact that man and his conditions were her main concerns.

Religion was "the center of Emily Dickinson's life," Skard argues. It was a religion of enormous dimensions--"Emerson's conceited belief in man was not for her."[13] To her, there were too many sides to God and his creations, some of which did not always seem good. Death has the same ambiguous quality--it is the "border where the worlds meet," something to long for and be wary of, at the same time.[14]

Briefly Skard discusses Dickinson's love poetry, for which he has the highest praise: it makes a stronger impression on the reader than "real" love poetry coming from almost any other poet.

Sigmund Skard, professor of American literature, University of Oslo, Norway, is well known as a poet and also as a translator of French, Latin, and American poetry.

[13]Skard, Stjerner, p. 21.

[14]Skard, Stjerner, p. 22.

Still, it is Dickinson's style which is revolutionary. Skard considers her superior to Emerson also in this respect: he compares her linguistic boldness and her unexpected imagery to that of Edward Taylor.

In 1961, Aagot Karner Smidt published an article mainly considering the status of Dickinson's poetry at the time.[15] Karner Smidt states that "it is no longer the right thing" to speak condescendingly of Dickinson as one of the few poets America has produced. Now, she is often considered the greatest woman poet in English literature and that statement may be more accurate. Karner Smidt pays particular tribute to Johnson's The Complete Poems of 1960 mainly because Dickinson readers can now read "the same" poems. She adds, however, that it would have been preferable to have had "a congenial poet" as editor of that book. Karner Smidt has only compliments for names such as Whicher, Leyda, and Anderson, whom she considers balanced and reliable Dickinson critics. However, Rebecca Patterson is dismissed with some ironic comments: "She [Dickinson] of course had to be homosexual just as Melville, Whitman, and all other first-rate artists."[16]

The latter part of the article is devoted to Karner Smidt's own comments on Dickinson's poetry. "For those who prefer final and dogmatic answers to the eternal questions of man, Emily Dickinson must seem . . . blasphemous. . . ."[17] But for those who do not get enough out of either religion, philosophy, or "common sense," Dickinson's poetry means inspiration and help. In fact, it "has to be the tension between belief and disbelief, between joy and grief, as well as between hope and

[15]Aagot Karner Smidt, "Emily Dickinson," Vinduet, [n. v.] (1961), pp. 220-23.

[16]Karner Smidt, p. 222.

[17]Karner Smidt, p. 223.

hopelessness that creates religious poetry; those secure in their beliefs can seldom give poetic life to their experiences," Karner Smidt concludes.[18] The name that leaps to one's mind in reading Dickinson is Kierkegaard, she adds as her final comment.

Between 1961 and 1968, the handful of Norwegian Dickinson critics published nothing on her. In 1968, however, in A History of English and American Literature for Schools, one finds somewhat more than a page devoted to Emily Dickinson.[19] The material contains the usual biographical background. The authors go on to call Dickinson "a poet of striking originality and significance." She treats "personal emotions and states of mind" and is called a pioneer in modern poetry, along with Whitman. Other than being the inspiration for "free verse," she is praised for her "genuine artistic instinct" that made her find beauty--and significance--in the simplest things in life, such as a bee's hum and other things in her garden. These everyday things provided her with metaphors for her themes.

Sigmund Skard is responsible for the part about American literature that appeared in Verdens litteraturhistorie [The Literary History of the World] in 1973.[20] The material is largely the

[18]Karner Smidt, p. 223.

[19]Lise Skabo and J. Meyer-Myklestad, A History of English and American Literature for Schools (Oslo: Gyldendal Norsk Forlag, 1968), pp. 147-48. The book is geared to higher schools, roughly comparable to senior high-school plus the first year of college in the United States.

[20]Sigmund Skard, "Emily Dickinson: Det analytiske auga" ["Emily Dickinson: The Analytical Eye"], Verdens litteraturhistorie (Oslo: Cappelens Forlag A. S., 1973), IV, 384-92. Subsequent references to this article will be cited as "Auga."

same as in his 1960 book, Under nye stjerner.
Some things have, of course, been added. For instance, the reader is informed that in the latter
part of the nineteenth century, Skard finds only
three first-rate American writers: Dickinson,
Henry James, and Mark Twain.[21] He compares Dickinson to Carlyle, Elizabeth Barrett, and George
Eliot, but finds that those three do not measure
up to Dickinson. Her "intellectual humor" Skard
now compares to "an Emerson dancing on his hands."
Skard obviously still considers Emerson inferior
to Dickinson.[22] Skard has expanded his comments
on Dickinson's "surrealistic" language; her poetry
today hits the reader with much more force than it
could have ever done in the nineteenth century, he
concludes. "She speaks of her name eventually being covered up by moss. Never has that time seemed further away."[23]

       An anonymous reporter interviewed Inger Hage-
rup in Vinduet in 1974.[24] The interview treats
Hagerup's career as a poet from its beginning in
1939.[25] Asked about her own favorite poets, Hagerup states that there are many women among them,
first of all Emily Dickinson. Hagerup sees Emily
Dickinson as "enormously neurotic," on account of
the "terrifying milieu" she lived in--"talk about
a man's world."[26] Hagerup places Dickinson's love

       [21]Skard, "Auga," p. 384.

       [22]Skard, "Auga," pp. 385-86.

       [23]Skard, "Auga," p. 392.

       [24][Interview], Vinduet [n. v.] (1974), pp.
28-40.

       [25]At this time, 1939, much of Hagerup's poet-
ry was politically oriented; this was right before
the German invasion of Norway in 1940.

       [26][Interview], p. 37.

poetry particularly high, written to "somebody she could not have. . . . And why she could not have him, that's exciting--to keep wondering about."[27] Hagerup, at the end of the article, compares Dickinson to some Swedish poets, in particular Karin Boye.[28]

Following this interview, Vinduet includes "Emily Dickinson: Elleve dikt" ["Emily Dickinson: Eleven Poems"] translated by Hagerup.[29] Four poems had been published in Hagerup's translation before.

Immediately following these poems, Vinduet, in what amounts to almost a Dickinson issue, includes an article by Hagerup simply entitled "Emily Dickinson."[30] It starts with the before-mentioned poem dedicated to Emily Dickinson, "Meget spinkel. Meget liten."[31] Emily Dickinson, Hagerup declares, is obviously one of America's greatest poets, or, "according to many, the very greatest." It is significant that the break-through of Dickinson's poetry did not come before 1924, thirty-eight years after the death of the

[27][Interview], p. 37.

[28]Karin Boye, renowned Swedish woman poet who committed suicide in 1941.

[29]Inger Hagerup, "Emily Dickinson: Elleve dikt," Vinduet, [n.v.] (1974), pp. 41-42. Some of the other poems are: "I felt a Funeral, in my Brain"; "What is--'Paradise'"; "Safe in their Alabaster Chambers"; "You said that I 'was Great' --one Day"; and "A little Madness in the Spring."

[30]Inger Hagerup, "Emily Dickinson," Vinduet, [n. v.] (1974), pp. 43-46. Since this is the second article of the same title by Hagerup, any subsequent reference will be cited in full, "Emily Dickinson."

[31]Cf. footnote 11.

poet, Hagerup observes. But the world was not ready for her poetry before. One finds in her poetry, Hagerup argues, a proud "either-or" mentality where the soul indeed selects its own society. This "either-or" mentality lets the soul in for many a defeat, or loss, and it is as a poet of defeat that Dickinson belongs among the greatest poets in the world. She could not rebel on the outside; instead the sparks of her feelings explode in poetry. And they explode not only in poetry, Hagerup adds, because Dickinson's letters have to be placed on the same level of quality. They, too, served as an outlet much needed. "Resignation in the ordinary sense of the word does not exist in the poetry of Emily Dickinson--she is beyond that. She is never relaxed,"[32] Hagerup maintains. One moment she may "stare through the centuries" and the next moment she may study a flower in her garden. Finally, Hagerup comes back to Dickinson's particular sense of time: Dickinson probably knew that the power of her poetry was strong enough to carry her into the future--some time, some place.[33]

This article marks the end of Norwegian criticism and translations (Hagerup and Skard) of Emily Dickinson through the year 1977. Two M.A. theses have been written in Norway, one of which will be considered here.[34] Dagny Blom wrote

[32]Hagerup, "Emily Dickinson," p. 45.

[33]Cf. Hagerup's discussion of time, p. 67.

[34]Dagny Blom, "Sea, Sun, and Noon: A Study of Three Symbols in Emily Dickinson's Poetry," M.A. Thesis University of Oslo, 1976. The other unpublished thesis is Liv Reidun Kjørsvik's "Religion in the Life and Poetry of Emily Dickinson," M.A. Thesis University of Oslo, 1956. As the title indicates, this thesis treats the concepts of God and death in Dickinson's poetry, in addition to giving the poet's New England background.

"Sea, Sun, and Noon: A Study of Three Symbols in Emily Dickinson's Poetry." The project is an ambitious one. Blom states that "the following chapters on the sea, sun, and noon symbols will elaborate on the assumption that the quest for fulfillment, the movement from a state of tragic separation towards a state of reunion and wholeness, is the primary concern of the poetess in her world."[35] All through the thesis, Blom stresses what she considers the plight of women in any time period: "I believe that the fact that Emily Dickinson was a woman calls for special attention. A female writer in the nineteenth century as well as now, writes under conditions which are different from those of a man. It is important to understand her writing in relation to the conditions created by an oppressive, male-dominated world."[36]

According to Blom, the sea has a wide range of meanings in Dickinson's poetry. It can stand for love, rebirth, and immortality; it can also stand for death, despair, or the mystery of living in general. Blom pays tribute to Inder Nath Kher when he suggests that in Dickinson, imagination has its roots in the sea, because the sea encompasses all of existence.[37]

The sun, on the other hand, is said to represent compensation if one is separated from the sun; if one is reconciled with it, the sun connotes grace and immortality. Overall, Blom considers "Dickinson's attitude toward the sun analogous to her attitude toward the male."[38]

[35]Blom, p. 3.

[36]Blom, p. 4.

[37]Inder Nath Kher, The Landscape of Absence: Emily Dickinson's Poetry (New Haven: Yale University Press, 1974), p. 104, as cited in Blom, p. 38.

[38]Blom, p. 62.

Blom describes noon as a personal and private symbol; thus, it can be a positive symbol, for instance connoting ecstasy, but also a negative one, meaning separation. In her conclusion, Blom identifies the first two symbols as "male lovers."[39] In the same vein, Blom calls noon the symbol of "fulfilment."[40]

Finally, as an indicator of the status of Emily Dickinson around 1970, one may look at the entry of a well-known Norwegian reference book, Aschehougs Konversasjonsleksikon.[41] What Dickinson's contemporaries were unable to appreciate was her "original language" and "bold ideas, in particular when she wrote about God or death." In the short bibliography, all of Thomas H. Johnson's books are referred to, together with Charles Anderson's Emily Dickinson's Poetry: Stairway of Surprise (New York: Holt, Rinehart and Winston, 1960).

Norway's southern neighbor, Denmark, has paid comparatively little attention to Emily Dickinson--the word "comparatively" is used advisedly because the country, after all, has only some five million inhabitants. Also, Denmark traditionally has favored prose over poetry, possibly because it has always had a politically powerful, commercially-oriented middle class.[42] It is perhaps indicative of this modest reception that the first time Emily Dickinson is mentioned in Denmark is in a

[39]Blom, p. 106.

[40]Blom, p. 107.

[41]Aschehougs Konversasjonsleksikon [Aschehoug's Conversation Dictionary] (Oslo: H. Aschehoug og Co., 1969), IV, 771.

[42]Indeed, culturally and sociologically, Denmark has always offered more parallels to England than to its Scandinavian neighbors.

footnote.[43] In the six lines devoted to her, one is informed that "the form of her poetry shows insecurity" but yet it has appealed to modern readers because of its simple and natural language, as well as its "clear images."[44] However, tribute is paid to "the genuine quality of the content" of Dickinson's poetry. In the last sentence, "an obscure love experience" is mentioned, and, and, concludes Møller, "it has not reduced the interest in her."

The second time Emily Dickinson is mentioned in Denmark is important for two reasons.[45] First, Paul Sørensen's article was the introduction of Emily Dickinson to the Danish public. Second, the article contains the very first translations of Emily Dickinson into Danish, almost a dozen poems. The translations are Sørensen's own. "In 1886," the author begins, "the greatest woman poet in English" died. He goes on to observe that without a doubt she is one of the poets who has had an enormous influence on modern and even recent poetry. The form of her poetry is brief, clear, and simple, in a highly sophisticated way. Sørensen argues that "the love of half-rhymes [among English-speaking poets] dates from her."[46] It is the very same simplicity that has kept the classics timeless through the centuries that is typical of Emily Dickinson's poetry: there is only place for

[43]Niels Møller, Verdens Litteraturen [World Literature] (København: Gyldendalske Boghandel Nordisk Forlag, 1929), p. 687. E. A. Robinson is the poet to whom Emily Dickinson is briefly compared in a six-line footnote.

[44]Møller, p. 687.

[45]Paul Sørensen, "Emily Dickinsons Digte" ["Emily Dickinson's Poetry"], Berlingske Aftenavis, December 15, 1950, Kronik pp. 6, 8.

[46]Sørensen, Kronik p. 6.

what is important and for none of those details
that might change with time and technical development. It is Sørensen's opinion that "through all
of her poetry, there runs a deep, secure, and
child-like belief in God."[47] The author's example
of this is "Aldrig saa jeg en Hede" ["I never saw
a Moor"]. Among other translations in the article
are some of the most often encountered: "To Gange
var mit Liv forbi" ["My life closed twice"];
"Sjaelen vaelger sit eget Selskab" ["The Soul selects her own Society"]; and "Der findes et Vinter-
skraalys" ["There's a certain Slant of light"].[48]
Sørensen ends his article in the hope that the
Danish public will soon take a serious interest in
"a great and modern poet unknown here at home."

Despite this hopeful last sentence of Søren-
sen's, nothing was written in Denmark on Emily
Dickinson between 1950 and 1965. The only excep-
tion is two poems translated, but not commented on,
by Ove Abildgaard in 1960. The two poems are
"Sejren" ["Success is counted sweetest"] and
"Fangen" ["Surgeons must be very careful"].[49]
Sørensen in 1965 was the first to turn to Emily
Dickinson, this time in his Moderne Amerikansk
Lyrik: Fra Whitman til Sandburg [Modern American
Poetry: From Whitman to Sandburg].[50] Sørensen re-
marks that even if one would not--as has been

[47]Sørensen, Kronik p. 8.

[48]Some other titles are: "I never lost as
much but twice"; "Elysium is as far as to"; and
"To fight aloud, is very brave."

[49]Ove Abildgaard, "To dikte af Emily Dickinson: 'Sejren' og 'Fangen'" ["Two Poems by Emily
Dickinson: 'Success is counted sweetest' and 'Surgeons must be very careful'"], Aktuelt, 10 (1960),
30.

[50]Paul Sørensen, "Emily Dickinson," Moderne
Amerikansk Lyrik: Fra Whitman til Sandburg

done[51]--call Emily Dickinson the greatest woman poet in English, one would always have to regard her as a first-rate poet. The quality of her poetry stems from a certain tension, namely that between her "boring," provincial physical surroundings and the span of her soul, a soul that sees beyond continents and centuries. Her physical person is small--her soul encompasses everything. Sørensen maintains that behind the outer form of simple four-line stanzas, there is a truthfulness without compromises. Her imagery is as exact as it is novel: in this respect, one might compare her to Edward Taylor or John Donne. However, it is Sørensen's opinion that Dickinson's imagery is richer and of a wider range than theirs.

Sørensen goes on to discuss some reasons why Emily Dickinson's poetry seems timeless. First, "poetry of today is heavily influenced by Emily Dickinson and therefore it constantly reminds us of her."[52] Also, Dickinson never writes about the fringes of the human experience but only about central problems that concern us all.

Sørensen devotes the latter part of his critical introduction to form; he sees some common denominators in Emerson and Dickinson, although he considers Dickinson vastly superior. He goes on to divide poets into roughly two groups: the ones that use words "as upholstery" and the ones that make "content part of the structure of the language."[53] To the first group he counts, among others mentioned, Poe, Emerson, and Whitman. In

---

(København: Borgens Billigbøger, 1960), pp. 152-73. Subsequent references to this article will be cited as "Emily Dickinson."

[51]Among others, by Sørensen himself, in 1950.

[52]Sørensen, "Emily Dickinson," p. 153.

[53]Sørensen, "Emily Dickinson," p. 171.

the latter group belong Stephen Crane, Pound, and, above all, Emily Dickinson. Sørensen hastens to add that the second type of poets is "not necessarily" of better quality, but in general that would be the case. Sørensen effectively uses the German saying <u>Zeichnen ist weglassen</u> to illustrate the point that it is often what is not said, rather than what is said, that makes for the explosive and powerful quality of such poetry as Dickinson's.[54]

Brevity in Dickinson's poetry, Sørensen argues, is mostly of the Latin variety, for instance in the kind of vocabulary that was the product of centuries of Roman influence. This Latin influence constitutes the "very spine of Dickinson's poetry," Sørensen continues. It is the condensed quality of her poetry, whether in vocabulary or otherwise, that makes this high-powered poet particularly suitable for being read in small doses. Added to the introduction are fifty of Dickinson's poems in Sørensen's translation.

In 1966, Ernst Dupont and Peter M. Cummings published <u>24 American Poets from Bryant to the Present</u>.[55] The book is geared to young students and pretends to be no more than a brief introduction to each poet.[56] Emily Dickinson's poems, the authors maintain, are "similar to Greek epigrams,

[54] <u>Zeichnen ist weglassen</u> = "to draw is to leave out."

[55] Ernst Dupont and Peter M. Cummings, <u>24 American Poets from Bryant to the Present</u> (København: G. E. C. Gads Forlag, 1966), pp. 40-44. Six poems are quoted in the book: "Success is counted sweetest"; "Elysium is as far as to"; "As imperceptibly as Grief"; "Because I could not stop for Death"; "I died for Beauty"; and "'Hope' is the thing with feathers."

[56] The readers would correspond to senior high-school and freshman students in the U.S.A.

being short, serious, economical, and ending with a precise or ironic statement about experience."[57] Her use of metaphors is exquisite and there is the typical Dickinsonian dichotomy between simple language and the mysteries of human life. Typical also is her use of concrete objects to convey an abstract experience. Then follow six of Dickinson's poems to illustrate the points made in the introduction.

Sigmund Skard's contribution to the Norwegian Verdens litteraturhistorie, i.e., his chapter on Emily Dickinson, is part of the translation of this whole book from Norwegian into Danish.[58] Skard's text, of course, is virtually the same as in the original Norwegian and need not be commented on here. The only thing worth pointing out, because it may not be immediately obvious to an English-speaking reader, is the fact that a Norwegian book needs translation into Danish, however closely related these languages might be.

There remains only to be considered a well-known Danish reference book testifying to Emily Dickinson's reputation around 1970.[59] "Emily Dickinson, along with Walt Whitman, is the foremost poet of America. Her language is simple and sublime; she has a decidedly strong sense of humor together with an ability to put down complicated reflections in a witty way,"[60] says the

[57]Dupont and Cummings, p. 40.

[58]Sigmund Skard, "Emily Dickinson - det analytiske øje," Verdens litteraturhistorie [The Literary History of the World], ed. Per Nykrog (København: Politikens Forlag, 1973), IX, 387-95.

[59]Henning Fonsmark, ed., Verdens Litteraturen: Hvem skrev hvad før 1914 [The World Literature: Who Wrote What before 1914] (København: Politikens Forlag, 1969), pp. 157-58.

[60]Fonsmark, p. 158.

anonymous writer. She writes about the simple
things of everyday living but also about more profound problems such as loneliness and death. The
one bibliographical piece of information given refers to Löfmarck's Swedish book of 1950.

Summary of Norwegian-Danish Criticism of

Emily Dickinson

In Norway, then, only the poet-critic Inger
Hagerup published on Emily Dickinson before Paal
Brekke in 1957. On the other hand, there is no
question of slow, or growing, interest in Dickinson but rather of a deep appreciation established
already the first time the poet is mentioned.
Inger Hagerup published three times on Dickinson
in the forties. Her first article stresses the
timeless quality of Dickinson's themes; all-human
topics such as nature, love, and death tend to inspire rereading of the poetry (see footnote 2).
This article also contains the first two Dickinson poems translated into Norwegian. A year later,
Hagerup published two more poems, one a reprint
from 1943 and one a new translation (see footnote
5). At the end of the decade, Hagerup, in another
article, states that it is her opinion that the
qualities found in Dickinson's poetry are to be
found in the production of no other poet (see footnote 6). Also in this article, Hagerup concentrates on what she considers to be Dickinson's
view of time, and perhaps, therefore, of fame.
Another four poems in Hagerup's translation mark
the end of the 1949 article.

In all of the next decade, only one poet-critic published on Emily Dickinson. Paal Brekke's
Amerikansk lyrikk: Et utvalg i norsk gjendiktning
is a full-length book including poetry from Whitman to Pound (see footnote 9). That Brekke considers Dickinson the most important poet is testified to by the fact that she is represented by
more poems than anyone else. Brekke stresses
Dickinson's "unequalled" handling of irony and
paradox, as well as her "aphoristic virtuosity."

78

The sixties saw three publications on Dickinson. Of these, two were books. Sigmund Skard's Under nye stjerner treats 300 years of American poetry (see footnote 12). He stresses Dickinson's "revolutionary" linguistic means to convey what concerned her the most: the different aspects of dying and of losing in a love relationship. Skard considers Dickinson superior even to Emerson, both in language and imagery.

Aagot Karner Smidt published an article which starts out as an over-view of Dickinson criticism (see footnote 15). She devotes the latter part of the article to specific aspects of Dickinson's poetry: the absence of "easy" or dogmatic answers to man's eternal questions, and the tension between joy and grief that is the mark of outstanding religious poetry. Karner Smidt finally compares Dickinson to Kierkegaard, certainly a compliment of the highest order.

The last item of the decade was Skabo-Myklestad's A History of English and American Literature for Schools (see footnote 19). The book is interesting mainly for one reason: young people are now exposed to Dickinson's poetry on a regular basis. Despite the limited space, the authors manage to convey their high regard for Dickinson as a pioneer in modern poetry.

Five items were published in the seventies (as of 1977). Of these, three had to do with Hagerup: one was an interview with her treating in particular her interest in Dickinson; one consisted of eleven Dickinson poems translated by Hagerup; and, finally, one was an article on Dickinson by Hagerup.

Sigmund Skard opened this decade of Dickinson criticism by including an essay on Dickinson in a literary history, Verdens litteraturhistorie (see footnote 20). He still holds the same views both of the linguistic skill of Dickinson, which he considers superior to Emerson's, and of her pro-

found insight into human problems; in the nineteenth century, only Henry James and Mark Twain
are of comparable quality, he maintains.

The 1944 interview with Inger Hagerup stresses
Hagerup's evaluation of Dickinson's influence in
her own life; among several poets judged first-
rate, Dickinson is called the foremost (see footnote 24). Hagerup's distaste for Dickinson's New
England background is stated openly; so is her admiration for the individual who could use that
background to produce first-rate poetry. After
giving her translations of eleven poems (see footnote 29), Hagerup published an article on Dickinson (see footnote 30). As in the interview,
Hagerup's concern is still mainly with the psychology of a poet who was far ahead of her time
and yet apparently was convinced of the carrying-
power of her own poetry. The Puritan environment
would not let Dickinson rebel openly against conventions; instead, her poetry provided a world in
which her originality could bloom.

Dagny Blom, in her unpublished 1976 thesis,
concentrated on the "male-dominated" world of
Dickinson (see footnote 34). Blom never mentions
Freud but her reading of the sea and the sun as
"male lovers" is only one example of many that
would put the thesis in the category of Freudian
interpretation.

What holds true for the Norwegian Dickinson
criticism, namely the fact that virtually everything is appreciative of the poet, does not quite
hold true for Denmark. Of the handful of items
published in this country, the first one, a footnote, was unfavorable (see footnote 43). In this
footnote of 1929, the reader is informed that the
form of Dickinson's poetry shows "insecurity,"
even if her imagery is appealing. The fact that
twenty-one years passed before Paul Sørensen published his "Emily Dickinsons Digte" in 1950 might
explain the definite change in attitude toward the
poet: now there is no doubt as to Dickinson being

"the greatest woman poet in English" (see footnote 45). Sørensen pays tribute both to Dickinson's role as a forerunner of "modern" poetry and her "simplicity" in general, a simplicity which explains her timelessness, according to him. Sørensen adds several translations of Dickinson poems to his article, the first ones to be published in Danish.

Sørensen's 1965 publication, <u>Moderne Amerikansk Lyrik</u>, offered little new (see footnote 50). He has, however, expanded his discussion of Dickinson's language. Commenting on the poet's imagery, he now places her above John Donne and Edward Taylor.

Finally in 1966, <u>24 American Poets from Bryant to the Present</u> was published, a book comparable to the Skabo-Myklestad publication in Norway (see footnote 55). The importance of the book lies in the fact that Dickinson's poetry is now part of the ordinary high-school education in Denmark. The book contains six poems by Dickinson in addition to the critical comments.

Thus, only a few items have been published on Dickinson in Denmark, two by the same author. Compared to its Scandinavian neighbors, Denmark has shown little interest in Dickinson. Considering the fact that Denmark has produced more prose than poetry as well as devoted more scholarly criticism to prose than to poetry, the scarcity of Dickinson material is perhaps not surprising. Contrary to this tendency, Sweden, for instance, has traditionally shown a significant interest in poetry. So has the next country to be considered in drawing the picture of Emily Dickinson in Europe, France, a nation traditionally appreciative of the woman-artist.

IV. France and French-speaking Switzerland

One need only think of the French institution of the <u>salon littéraire</u> so common already in the seventeenth century to realize some of the importance of women in French intellectual circles. The tradition of informal gatherings in the home of the woman-artist--gatherings subtly guided by and strongly influenced by this artist-hostess-- well deserves to be called an institution: the <u>salon littéraire</u> has been the most appreciated way for intellectuals and artists in France to exchange ideas ever since. Gertrude Stein's <u>salon</u> for her "lost generation" was nothing but a follow-up of a time-honored tradition. In addition to the general standing of the woman-artist in France, many things converged in the twenties which might explain the early appreciation of Emily Dickinson's poetry in this country. After World War I, the French had had enough of "action," whether in reality or literature. People wanted to read more with a view toward an understanding of man's inner life than of his actual outward actions. The almost desperate desire to turn away from the everyday business of living toward the rewarding business of reading is testified to by the unprecedented prosperity that the French publishing houses were enjoying in the twenties. As Roger Asselineau points out in <u>The Literary Reputation of Hemingway in Europe</u>, the French reading public showed a new interest in what was going on in other countries.[1] So the way was prepared for foreign writers, in particular those from countries that had now emerged as world powers. Translations were more numerous than ever before. Also

---

[1] Roger Asselineau, "French Reactions to Hemingway's Works between the Two World Wars," <u>The Literary Reputation of Hemingway in Europe</u>, ed. Roger Asselineau (New York: New York University Press, 1965), pp. 50-54, 57, 59.

at this time, the first two academic chairs in American literature were created in Paris and Lyon to meet the demand of an expanded interest in American culture.[2]

During this decade of general pessimism in France, the twenties, a general preference for the non-conformist writer became increasingly obvious. As Asselineau has pointed out, the appreciation of the individual became more significant and, perhaps as a consequence, so did the preoccupation with individual style.[3] In fact, contrary to the situation in many other countries, the French literary climate was ready for the poetry of Emily Dickinson in the mid-twenties.

1925 was the year of the first French publication on Dickinson. The critic was a specialist in the field of American literature, Jean Catel, and the article was "Emily Dickinson: Essai d'analyse psychologique" ["Emily Dickinson: An Attempt at a Psychological Analysis"].[4] Professor Catel begins his article by stating that "Emily has never enjoyed, up to now, the reputation she deserves." Catel proceeds to defend psychoanalysis as a means of literary evaluation: the application of this method in evaluation of literature is rare, he observes, but the works of poets and novelists lend themselves particularly well to psychoanalysis. The writers, Catel maintains, often write because of a neurosis; they shy away from the realities of living. Catel's article is tightly argued. His first example of writers who never freed themselves from the paternal influ-

[2]Asselineau, p. 54.

[3]Asselineau, p. 57.

[4]Jean Catel, "Emily Dickinson: Essai d'analyse psychologique," Revue Anglo-Américaine, 2 (June 1925), 394-405. Subsequent references to this article will be cited as "Analyse psychologique."

ence is Charlotte Brontë, but Dickinson is an
even "better example." Catel discusses in detail
the stern aspects of Edward Dickinson's character;
nevertheless, he adds, it is obvious that "Emily
adored her father."[5] Later on, Catel continues,
Emily's teachers became the focal points for her
affections since they represented authority. At
South Hadley, Emily was desolate--logically so,
according to Catel, since she was separated from
her father. Still, Catel continues his Freudian
character reading, Emily was not yet a victim of
"repressed desires."[6] The "substitution"--in
Freud's sense--takes place when Emily met the man
who "could deliver her from her father complex."
The identity of the beloved, Catel continues, is
still unknown to readers of Dickinson's poetry.
He remains the "substitution" until the correspondence with Colonel Higginson begins; the colonel
then becomes another substitution, although on a
different level. When Dickinson's father dies,
she dies too, Catel argues.[7] She had fought the
difficulties of living during a whole lifetime,
Catel concludes his article, only to be conquered
in the end. There remains only one victory: her
poetry. Without the use psychoanalytical methods
to read Emily Dickinson's subconscious, we would
not be able to understand "the flame of her poetry," Catel concludes.

Six months later, Catel published another
article in the same prestigious magazine.[8] In
"Emily Dickinson: L'oeuvre" ["Emily Dickinson: The

[5]Catel, "Analyse psychologique," p. 396.

[6]Catel, "Analyse psychologique," p. 398.

[7]Catel, "Analyse psychologique," p. 404.

[8]Jean Catel, "Emily Dickinson: L'oeuvre,"
Revue Anglo-Américaine, 3 (December 1925), 105-
20. Subsequent references to this article will
be cited as "L'oeuvre."

85

Work"], Catel first pays tribute to Dickinson's intellectual power; the modern poets, he adds, have every reason to "salute their master." To Dickinson, reality is mainly beauty--the beauty of little things--at least when she does not write about death. Among some of the most successful poems, Catel mentions "Nature--the Gentlest Mother is"; "Will there really be a 'Morning'?"; "Angels, in the early morning"; "To hear an Oriole sing"; "To my quick ear the Leaves--conferred"; and "It cant be 'Summer.'" Some of the "beauty" is better called "mirage," Catel continues. Such is the feeling of peace which Dickinson seeks but, as a true artist, never finds. As examples, Catel offers "I many times thought Peace had come"; "There is a solitude of space"; and "Beauty crowds me till I die." Out of "There is a solitude of space," Catel chooses the line "a soul admitted to itself" to show the core of her poetry. Her whole work, he believes, is only a variation of this one theme, sometimes happy, and sometimes sombre. Catel finds her whole education, her "anti-romantic instinct," as well as "the pride of her Puritan conscience" embedded in this theme.[9]

Catel argues that death provides another preoccupation for Dickinson. At Amherst, everybody knew everybody and the thought of death was a constant companion. According to Catel, Dickinson sees the grave as "a passage" only; the real home lies beyond. Is Emily a genuine Christian? Hardly, Catel answers; in her whole poetic output, one looks in vain for anything but "a vague belief," prompted by "natural phenomena."[10] Also, Catel adds, the condemnation of sinners and severe lecturing associated with the Puritan religion in Amherst could hardly but offend Emily, rather than inspire a true belief in God. Her religious poetry is such that "an anti-religious magazine would have welcomed it," maintains Catel, "but then there

[9]Catel, "L'oeuvre," p. 111.

[10]Catel, "L'oeuvre," p. 114.

was no such thing at Amherst."[11] Nevertheless, Catel believes, in some fashion she believed in a God, "fatal and good at the same time." Catel reminds the reader that "the yearning to return to the womb," typical of her kind of neurosis, explains her particular brand of religion.[12] He argues that Emily, in order to survive in her frustrating world, attempted to view life, even religion, with humor. "Papa above!" is quoted as a typical example, one out of many such poems.

In attempting to sum up the qualities of Dickinson's poetry, Catel is not altogether positive. The poet is, according to him, "purely intellectual" and, therefore, "something is missing in her work." She is "far away from real life" and "made of a marble that is cold to the touch."[13] Despite this statement, he goes on to say that her "intellectual vision rarely surpasses that of the ordinary man," but she does have something that we should not forget: the sincerity of her emotions. In this regard, she has an advantage over us modern human beings with our love for obscurity, rare words, and generally "tortured" expressions, Catel concludes his article. It is worth noticing that Catel incorporates partial translations of Dickinson poems--phrases, lines, or one stanza--into his argument. Only one brief poem is given in a complete translation: "O mon coeur, oublions-le!" ["Heart! We will forget him!"].

Régis Michaud,[14] author of numerous full-length critical works on American literature, in

[11]Catel, "L'oeuvre," p. 114.

[12]Cf. Catel's inclination toward Freudian readings as manifested in the preceding article.

[13]Catel, "L'oeuvre," p. 120.

[14]Among Michaud's many critical works, the following are to be found: Mystiques et Réalistes

87

1926 devoted limited space to Emily Dickinson in
his Panorama de la Littérature Américaine Contemporaine [Panorama of Contemporary American
Literature].[15] Michaud's first comment on Dickinson is reminiscent of Catel ("a soul admitted to
itself"). Not only is introspection Dickinson's
muse, argues Michaud, but this muse appears "ab-
solutely naked in Emily Dickinson's poetry."[16] On
the whole, Michaud is appreciative of Dickinson's
"quarrel with destiny." He finds in her poetry
"an odor of prison but they [the poems] are illuminated by thought."[17] We are far away from romantic declamations and the artifices of a Longfellow,
Michaud continues. "A whole school of poets will
recognize itself in this laconism" is Michaud's
final remark.

1927 saw the last Dickinson publication of
the twenties. Albert Feuillerat published "La Vie
Secrète d'Une Puritaine: Emily Dickinson" ["The
Secret Life of a Puritan: Emily Dickinson"].[18]

Anglo-Saxons [Anglo-Saxon Mystics and Realists];
La Pensée Américaine: Autour d'Emerson [American
Thought: The Circle Around Emerson]; Le Roman
Américain d'Aujourd'hui: Critique d'une Civilisation
[The American Novel of Today: Critique of a
Civilization]; and L'esthétique d'Emerson [The
Esthetics of Emerson]. Le Roman Américain was
awarded a prize by l'Académie française.

[15]Régis Michaud, Panorama de la Littérature
Américaine Contemporaine (Paris: Simon Kra, 1926),
pp. 128-29, 182, 226. Subsequent references to
this book will be cited as Panorama.

[16]Michaud, Panorama, p. 128.

[17]Michaud, Panorama, p. 129.

[18]Albert Feuillerat, "La Vie Secrète d'Une
Puritaine: Emily Dickinson," Revue des Deux Mondes,

A major part of the article is devoted to tracing, in detail, all the aspects of Dickinson's Puritan upbringing. In such a milieu, Feuillerat argues, "repressed instincts liberate themselves," sooner or later. He sees some of this liberation in all three Dickinson children, but, above all, in Emily. She has "a teasing bend" to the point of being "indiscreet"; she is also a creature of passions. But not even she could free herself from her upbringing: Puritanism "with its efforts to kill the joys of life, its virtuous zeal apropos of nothing, and above all, its delicious conceit" was stronger than Emily, Feuillerat rather grimly adds.[19] Her one escape was poetry. Feuillerat considers the content of her poetry bold, even "nude," and finds her greatness in this quality. Feuillerat has nothing but praise for the "freshness" of her imagery and the elusive charm of even her most "difficult" poems. Her poetry, however, shows "no concern with technique" and the form is often faulty, according to him.[20] Feuillerat concludes his article by suggesting that in her later poetry, Dickinson grew more and more morbid. He cites no poems in support of this viewpoint but attributes this morbidity to the effects of Puritanism in general and also to the fact that most of Dickin-

---

40 (1927), 668-91. Among Professor Feuillerat's works are: John Lyly: Contribution à l'histoire de la Renaissance anglaise [John Lyly: Contribution to the History of the English Renaissance]; L'Histoire de théâtre de cour en Angleterre [History of the English Court Theatre]; Shakespeare: Collection des cent chefs-d'oeuvres étrangers [Shakespeare: A Collection of One Hundred Foreign Masterpieces]; Édition des oeuvres de Sir P. Sidney [An Edition of the Works of Sir P. Sidney]; and many others.

[19]Feuillerat, pp. 679-80.

[20]Feuillerat, p. 682.

son's loved ones had died at this point in her
life.[21]

Léon Bocquet's "La Littérature Américaine"
["American Literature"] is of interest in a Dickinson study for one specific reason: Emily Dickinson is mentioned as one of the few first-rate
artists in a literature not yet out of its "tod-
dling years."[22] It is Professor Bocquet's opinion that no literature worthy of the name existed
in the United States before the Civil War; biographies and sociological writings are of value only
in the sense that they helped create a nation,

[21]An M.A. thesis was written in 1938 on,
among other things, the French response to Emily
Dickinson: Katherine Kenyon Stewart, "French Criticism of Four American Poets: Poe, Whitman, Dickinson, Robinson," M.A. Thesis University of Kansas
1938. Erroneously, Miss Stewart considers the
French response to Dickinson "decidedly limited"
(p. 87) and she goes on to say: "Only two French
critics of consequence [Catel and Feuillerat] have
discussed Emily Dickinson" (p. 87), disregarding
even a name such as Régis Michaud as well as other
critical items published in the thirties before
1938. The actual praise of both Catel and Feuillerat
is understated in favor of their few negative comments. Thus, Miss Stewart concludes that "obviously, from the foregoing discussion, Emily Dickinson
has not yet been appreciated in France" (p. 101).
Miss Stewart sees two reasons for this lack of
appreciation: first, "she [Dickinson] did not
descend to the depths of feeling experienced by
Poe, nor did she soar to sublime heights" (p. 101).
Second, "she [Dickinson] wrote briefly and fanci-
fully on heart-rending subjects, and hence, her
poetry failed to appeal so greatly to men" (p.
101). Many critics, male or female, would disagree with Miss Stewart's viewpoints.

[22]Léon Bocquet, "La Littérature Américaine,"
Nouvelle Revue Critique, 15 (April 1931), 157-68.

Bocquet argues.[23] He admits, however, that "from the very beginning American literature has had its poets." But, he continues, "their voices . . . rise in the desert of general activity."[24] Among the poets mentioned is Emily Dickinson who "lived a secluded life in order to create a sincere and profound work whose merits went unnoticed until after the death of the poet."[25] To no other poet does Léon Bocquet pay a similar tribute in his survey.

John Jacoby in 1931 published his thought-provoking, although sometimes vague, "L'esthétique de la sainteté: Emily Dickinson," in Le Mysticisme dans la Pensée Américaine [Mysticism in American Thought].[26] Jacoby sees Emily Dickinson as a true mystic; she is "the most exquisite product of American literature." He goes on to observe that she was "the toy of the grim spirit of that time" representing a rebellion against Puritan repression. Jacoby suggests that since "esthetic sensibilities" were not easy to develop in her surroundings, the best she could do was to draw back and watch life from a distance: "we have here the old problem of asceticism." Jacoby argues that during her whole life, Dickinson needed, as a consequence of this asceticism, "an intermediary person" to deal with people on any level, even with her father. In this solitude, she never doubted the existence of a God, although her brand of religion may sometimes seem irreverent. As an example of this viewpoint, Jacoby cites "Papa là-

[23]Bocquet, p. 158.

[24]Bocquet, p. 159.

[25]Bocquet, p. 162.

[26]John Jacoby, "L'esthétique de la sainteté: Emily Dickinson," Le Mysticisme dans la Pensée Américaine (Paris: Les Presses Universitaires de France, 1931), pp. 241-76.

haut! Regarde une Souris" ["Papa above!"].[27] As
a mystic, Dickinson regards pain as educational,
Jacoby suggests, because it "imposes sincerity."
Jacoby finds support for this opinion in "J'aime à
voir un air d'agonie" ["I like a look of Agony"].
The death poems are, of course, typical of the
mystic, Jacoby observes; however, he considers her
poems about nature the most successful. It is
only in these poems that we find the poet "within
the absolute power of inspiration." At this point,
Jacoby synthesizes what he considers to be the two
major ingredients of Dickinson's poetry: God and
nature. Jacoby suggests that the two are one. In
support of this view, Jacoby offers the following
translated poems: "Je goutte une boisson jamais
brassée" ["I taste a liquor never brewed"];[28] "Le
murmure d'une abeille" ["The Murmur of a Bee"]; and
"L'abeille n'a pas peur de moi." ["The Bee is
not afraid of me"]. Although it is an apparent
contradiction in terms, Jacoby concludes: "Emily
Dickinson was especially a nature mystic"; she saw
the meaning of life in physical nature. Others
may have other concerns, but "what she is, she is
to perfection. That is a pretty good passport to
immortality," Jacoby concludes.[29]

     In Revue des Cours et Conférences, Jean Catel
published an article mainly treating Whitman.[30]

     [27]As in the case of Catel, Jacoby translates
lines or stanzas of Dickinson poems. Rarely is a
poem translated in its entirety ("Papa above!" is
an exception, together with "Un peu de folie au
printemps" ["A little madness in the spring"]).

     [28]In partial translation.

     [29]Jacoby, p. 274.

     [30]Jean Catel, "Poésie moderne aux États-Unis
I," Revue des Cours et Conférences, 34 (May 15,
1933), 210-23. Subsequent references to this
article will be cited as "Poésie I."

It is in this article that Catel presents the
theory that poetry is a better medium to represent
life than any other.[31] Catel explains his theory
by discussing the often vague and fragmentary quality of our understanding of life--only poetry has
the properties to convey that quality. At the end
of the Whitman article, Catel pays tribute to Emily
Dickinson by observing that she, along with Whitman, also had "the instinct for poetry." These
two poets, Catel concludes, are proof that genuine
poetry has been produced within "this very new
nation [the United States]."

In the next issue of the same magazine, Catel
devoted an article to Dickinson.[32] In this article, Catel attempts to categorize Dickinson's poetry and supplies examples by quoting several poems
in his own translation.[33] The first of Catel's
categories is "the little things" in life and his
example is "La beauté m'assaille jusqu' à mourir"
["Beauty crowds me till I die"]. To exemplify
"exterior nature," Professor Catel quotes, among
other poems, "Apportez-moi le couchant dans une
coupe" ["Bring me the sunset in a cup"]; "L'herbe
a si peu à faire" ["The Grass so little has to
do"]; and "Des anges au matin" ["Angels, in the
early morning"]. The seasons are celebrated in
"Cher Mars, entrez" ["Dear March--Come in"]. Finally, in Catel's section called "interior nature,"
the following two poems are discussed: "Coeur moins
lourd que le mien" ["Heart, not so heavy as mine"]
and "Avez-vous un ruisseau dans votre petit coeur?"
["Have you got a Brook in your little heart"].
Professor Catel was the first in France to use the

[31]Catel, "Poésie I," p. 212.

[32]Jean Catel, "Poésie moderne aux États-Unis
II," Revue des Cours et Conférences, 34 (May 30,
1933), 345-56.

[33]Again, mostly only parts of the poems have
been translated.

now familiar divisions of Dickinson's poetry, such
as nature poetry, death poetry, and so on. "Whitman . . . shouted; she murmured," Catel observes
at the end of his article. "Emily Dickinson . . .
is a Baudelaire, a Verlaine. . . . Walt Whitman is
a spontaneous poet," Professor Catel finally remarks. Coming from a Frenchman, this statement
implies a definite preference for Dickinson.

        The early French Dickinson criticism was
dominated by Jean Catel. In 1935, Catel published
yet another article, "Sur Emily Dickinson: A Propos
de Deux Livres" ["On Emily Dickinson: Apropos of
Two Books"].[34] The article provides brief comments on Josephine Pollitt's Emily Dickinson: The
Human Background of Her Poetry (New York: Harper
and Brothers, 1930), and Geneviève Taggard's The
Life and Mind of Emily Dickinson (New York: Alfred
A. Knopf, 1930). "We have just started to understand and love the unique work of Emily Dickinson
. . . who is probably the only genuine American
poet before modern poetry," Catel begins his article.[35] He goes on to say that there already exist many "adequate" critical commentaries on Dickinson's life and poetry, such as the two books by
Pollitt and Taggard. It is, however, Catel's
opinion that neither has given "irrefutable
proofs" as to the identity of Emily Dickinson's
beloved: according to Pollitt, it was a certain
Lieutenant Hunt; according to Taggard, it was
George Gould, a pastor. Catel argues that while
it is natural for a critic to try to solve any
biographical riddle, the outcome of such an attempt has little bearing on a correct interpretation of the work. "Particularly in the case of

        [34]Jean Catel, "Sur Emily Dickinson: A Propos
de Deux Livres," Revue Anglo-Américaine, 13 (December 1935), 140-44.

        [35]Cf. footnote 21 and Katherine Kenyon Stew-
art's comments on Catel's lack of appreciation of
Dickinson.

Emily Dickinson . . . the only universe she lived
in consists of the stanzas themselves," Catel
maintains.[36] He concludes his article by observing that the "admirable" work of Emily Dickinson
is like that of Donne, Keats, Browning, and Shakespeare. The biographical details of any artist may
intrigue the critic; this fact should not diminish
his love for their works.

The last publication on Dickinson of the decade was Pierre Leyris' "Poèmes et Lettres d'Emily
Dickinson" ["Poems and Letters of Emily Dickinson"].[37] Apart from the fragmentary translations
of selected lines or stanzas that had been part of
several longer critical articles up to this point,
Leyris is the first one to publish complete Dickinson poems in translation, six in all (in addition to some selected letters).[38] In his very
brief critical comments, Leyris suggests that
Emily Dickinson was, in part, influenced by Emerson; the only really close ties, however, were
with the English Metaphysical poets. Leyris humbly observes that the poems translated may not be
either the best or the most representative: they
are "simply the ones that the translator has not
altogether destroyed."

[36]Cf. chapter II, footnotes 100 and 150.
Emil Staiger argues along the same lines.

[37]Pierre Leyris, "Poèmes et Lettres d'Emily
Dickinson," Mesures, 5 (July 1939), 125-39.

[38]The six poems are: "L'eau, c'est la soif
qui l'apprend" ["Water, is taught by thirst"]; "Or
donc: la terre est brève" ["I reason, Earth is
short"]; "En hiver, dans ma chambre" ["In Winter
in my Room"]; "Au Jugement allé" ["Departed--to
the Judgment"]; "Espérant, craignais" ["When I
hoped I feared"]; and "Le spectacle, ce sont"
["The Show is not the Show"]. The edition of letters used is Mabel Loomis Todd, ed., Letters of
Emily Dickinson (New York: Harper and Brothers, 1931).

In 1945, Jean Catel again published on Emily Dickinson, including her along with other poets in a full-length book of translations, Quelques Poèmes de l'Amérique Moderne [Some Poems from Modern America].[39] Six poems by Dickinson are included, most of them in an abbreviated version.[40]

Also in 1945, Professor Charles Cestre published a literary history called La Littérature Américaine [American Literature].[41] The first paragraph of the chapter entitled "La Poésie" ["Poetry"] is of particular interest: "The end of the nineteenth century and the beginning of the twentieth saw a remarkable renaissance of poetry in America. There were two precursors of this renaissance, Emily Dickinson and William Vaughn Moody."[42] The inclusion of Moody, incidentally, is unusual: Dickinson and Whitman are the names most often encountered in this context. Professor Cestre attempts to define the particular qualities of Dickinson's poetry. In her less successful poems, he argues, one finds a "dryness" and a "monotony of form," but those poems are rare. In

[39]Jean Catel, Quelques Poèmes de l'Amérique Moderne (Paris: Collection Dauphine, 1945), pp. 12-13.

[40]The poems are: "Route d'evanescence" ["A Route of Evanescence"]; "C'était un tout petit bateau" ["'Twas such a little--little boat"]; "Oh! habiter dans des greniers superbes!" ["The Grass so little has to do"]; "L'âme est condamné à n'être" ["The Soul unto itself"]; "Où des bateaux de poupre oscillent" ["When Ships of Purple--gently toss"]; and "Oui, je m'enivre d'air pur" ["I taste a liquor never brewed"].

[41]Charles Cestre, La Littérature Américaine (Paris: Librairie Armand Colin, 1945), pp. 189-91. Subsequent references to this book will be cited as Littérature.

[42]Cestre, Littérature, p. 189.

96

general, one has to attribute to her "the gift of a genius." In her poetry, one finds elevated thoughts, an alert spontaneity, and a total sincerity, Cestre continues. He considers her love poetry her best: "She does not even hide her physical emotions behind the reserve of femininity."[43] However, Cestre finds the style and form of Dickinson's poetry even more impressive: everyday words are invested with noble ideas and the sentence structure is the simplest possible. Cestre observes that Dickinson "sacrifices the finished form to the suggestive form," a mode of expression that was hers alone at the time. Her "frankness and originality prefigure modern taste," Cestre concludes.[44]

Léonie Villard, in La Poésie Américaine: Trois Siècles de Poésie Lyrique et de Poèmes Narratifs [American Poetry: Three Centuries of Lyrical and Narrative Poetry] offered four poems in translation as well as critical comments.[45] After briefly treating Emerson and Whitman, she states: "The poet who gives us the supreme manifestation of a world vision . . . is a woman, Emily Dickinson." In her "untamed and voluntary" isolation, Dickinson manages to grasp "profound feelings," in fact, to go "straight to the core of the mystery of living." Villard argues that in her intuitive feeling for the immediate, Dickinson is a striking parallel to William Blake: both are visionaries. In support of this view, Villard cites "Je n'ai

[43]Cestre, Littérature, p. 190.

[44]Cestre, Littérature, p. 191. Cestre does not cite specific poems to illustrate his view.

[45]Léonie Villard, La Poésie Américaine: Trois Siècles de Poésie Lyrique et de Poèmes Narratifs (Paris: Bordas Frères, Les Éditions Françaises Nouvelles, 1945), pp. 77-84.

jamais vu une lande" ["I never saw a Moor"].[46] It
is Villard's opinion that Dickinson's voluntary
isolation is part of the reason why she is able to
judge life correctly; Dickinson is unrestricted by
the impositions of society.[47] Each of Dickinson's
poems, Villard concludes, arrives at its desti-
nation "without any verbal jugglery" or rhetoric.
With Dickinson, "we arrive at the doorstep of the
contemporary time period."

    In 1948, Charles Cestre published another
book on American literature, Les Poètes Américains
[The American Poets].[48] He again devotes much
space to Emily Dickinson. He is still of the o-
pinion that the form of her poetry is superior to
the content; despite the fact that she did not
"bother" about form as such, "she did not lack
artistic sense." Cestre observes that she helped
rejuvenate American poetry by stressing simplicity
and realism as well as by abandoning empty rhetorical mannerisms of the past. He adds: "Emily
Dickinson was sensitive to the union of verbal
sonority and profundity of thought."[49] As before,

    [46]The other poems are: "La souffrance a une
zone d'inconscience" ["Pain--has an Element of
Blank"]; "Une porte s'entrebâillait sur la rue"
["A Door just opened on a street"]; and "Le Paradis
est aussi loin" ["Elysium is as far as to"].
Villard's translations are the first complete ones
since Leyris' book; see footnote 37.

    [47]Cf. chapter II, footnotes 128 and 133,
where Ann-Marie Lund argues that Dickinson's isolation was "functional."

    [48]Charles Cestre, Les Poètes Américains
(Paris: Presses Universitaires de France, 1948),
pp. 91-103. Subsequent references to this book
will be cited as Poètes.

    [49]Cestre, Poètes, p. 97. Here Cestre differs
from many critics who have found Dickinson's poetry lacking in musicality.

Cestre places Dickinson's love poetry above the
other kinds and, again, he pays tribute to the
fact that she "forgets the prudence of the Puritan
moral code and the timidity of her sex. She cries
out her desire to become a woman."[50] Cestre's example is "Nuits éperdues! nuits éperdues!" ["Wild
Nights--Wild Nights!"].[51] All is novel and personal in Dickinson's poetry, Cestre maintains: the
form, the feelings, and the thoughts. "The creative force . . . reveals her [Dickinson's] gran-
deur," Cestre concludes.

Also in 1948, Maurice Le Breton published
Anthologie de la Poésie Américaine Contemporaine
[Anthology of Contemporary American Poetry].[52] Le
Breton classifies Dickinson as an Imagist: "Before
the Imagists, and without intention, she proved
that one could, without rules, write poetry whose
charm lies not only in the perfect fusion between
image and object, but in the substitution of an
image . . . for the object itself."[53] Also, Le
Breton observes, she proved that suitable poetic
material is often near at hand--if this material
can be used in new ways. Protected by her isolation from "the contagion" of the low-quality poetry of her contemporaries, she managed to keep
"her spirit free from Puritan narrowmindedness and

[50]Cestre, Poètes, p. 99.

[51]As in the cases of Catel and others, Cestre,
in most cases, offers only partial translations.
Some of the poems are: "Il faut le malheur" ["Must
be a Wo"]; "La qualité immaterielle de ceux" ["The
overtakelessness of those"]; and "Un coup de mort
est un coup de vie pour ceux" ["A Death blow is a
Life blow to some"].

[52]Maurice Le Breton, Anthologie de la Poésie
Américaine Contemporaine (Paris: Éditions Denoël,
1948), pp. 35-38, 62-69. Subsequent references to
this book will be cited as Anthologie.

[53]Le Breton, Anthologie, p. 36.

her language from every cliché." To the Imagists,
Le Breton continues, she must have seemed, in all
senses, like a voice from the past authorizing the
audacity of the young. Dickinson had, Le Breton
concludes, "an extraordinary acuteness of vision
. . . [and] a quick sense of the precise line and
the precise word." The combination of "verbal
succinctness" and "malicious humor" is hers
alone.[54] Le Breton includes four poems, complete,
in translation.[55]

Jacques-Fernand Cahen's La Littérature
Américaine [American Literature] marked the beginning of a new decade which saw a dramatic increase
in Dickinson criticism.[56] Cahen comes close to Le
Breton in seeing Dickinson as a precursor of the
Imagists.[57] Cahen compares Stephen Crane to Dickinson but observes that Crane lacks "the charm"
and "the halo" of Dickinson. Contrary to many
critics, Cahen considers the form of Dickinson's
poetry "elegant" despite the fact that she followed the "caprices of her genius" only. Cahen remarks that her themes in themselves are far from
new; it is rather her "satire and humor" that explain the high level of poetic quality. Cahen
concludes that often there is a negative correla-
tion between the length and the quality of her

[54]Le Breton, Anthologie, p. 63.

[55]The four complete poems are: "Un être tout
en long dans l'herbe" ["A narrow Fellow in the
Grass"]; "Je hume un nectar non pareil" ["I taste
a liquor never brewed"]; "Si je n'étais plus en
vie" ["If I should'nt be alive"]; and "Je juge des
chanteurs d'après le Rouge-gorge" ["The Robin's
my Criterion for Tune"].

[56]Jacques-Fernand Cahen, La Littérature
Américaine (Paris: Presses Universitaires de
France, 1950), p. 72.

[57]Cf. footnote 52.

poems: the short ones are usually the best.

In 1951, Cyrille Arnavon published his Les
Lettres Américaines devant la Critique française
[American Literature in French Criticism].58 Professor Arnavon is less concerned with American
literature as such than with the quality of French
criticism, and, consequently, the title of the
book is slightly misleading. Emily Dickinson is
briefly mentioned: it took time, Arnavon observes,
for the critics to realize the value of Emily
Dickinson's poetry and Theodore Dreiser's novels.
Arnavon, who seldom gives high praise, applauds
critics such as Catel, Villard, Cestre, and, above
all, Régis Michaud.

Two years later, Professor Arnavon published
Histoire Littéraire des États-Unis [Literary History of the United States].59 Arnavon, as so many

58Cyrille Arnavon, "La Poésie Contemporaine
(1887-1917)," Les Lettres américaines devant la
Critique Française (Paris: Societé d'Édition "Les
Belles Lettres," 1951), pp. 123-36. One of the
values of this learned and witty history of French
criticism lies in the indirect proofs that Professor Arnavon provides for my suggestion that
Jean Catel was the first in France to publish on
Dickinson. Thus, for instance, Arnavon remarks
that, "with the exception of Régis Michaud's article on Moody" of 1911, not a single study in
France between 1887 and 1917 has been devoted to
"any major American poet" (p. 127). During the
"consecutive years," i.e., the twenties, Catel and
Villard, in addition to Michaud, "pushed the appreciation" of American literature (p. 134).
Arnavon also remarks that, "between 1915 and 1925,"
French criticism of American literature rests with
a handful of names (p. 142). Again, Michaud,
Catel, Villard, and Charles Cestre are the re-
current ones.

59Cyrille Arnavon, Histoire Littéraire des

101

others, places Dickinson in the tradition of the
Metaphysical poets observing that her work remains
foreign to the century in which she lived. "All
linguistic conventions are violated," Arnavon
notes, in the "nudity" of her expression; she
cares neither for "good taste" nor for musicality.[60] Her legacy to the Imagists lies in the fact
that she decreed the self as the one and only object for poetry, Arnavon concludes.

Because of Jean Simon, 1954 remains a landmark year in French Dickinson criticism.[61] Simon,
as the first one in France proper, published a
full-length book of Dickinson poems in translation, together with critical comments. The book
was entitled Emily Dickinson: Poèmes [Emily Dickinson: Poems].[62] After briefly noting that Dickinson, together with Whitman, would have to be considered the best poet America has produced, Professor Simon goes on to discuss Dickinson's "ideas"
versus her language. Some would call her a poet
of ideas, Simon remarks, but that evaluation is
hardly a valid one. Her ideas are "elementary"
and often "conventional," Simon argues. Nor does
her originality lie in her rhythm. Rather, it is
her language that makes her poetry immortal: she
chose her words as much for their sonority as for

États-Unis (Paris: Librairie Hachette, 1953), p.
355. Subsequent references to this book will be
cited as Histoire.

[60]Arnavon, Histoire, p. 355.

[61]Jean Simon is a professor at the Sorbonne
and author of numerous studies on American literature, for instance on Melville and on the nineteenth-century novel.

[62]Emily Dickinson: Poèmes, trans. and introd.
Jean Simon (Paris: Pierre Seghers, 1954).

their meaning.[63]   It is "the words and images that
constitute the life of her poems."   She remains as
"advanced" a poet for our time as she was considered, for instance, at the time of the Imagists,
Simon concludes.

Also in 1954, André Maurois,[64] member of
l'Académie française and one of the most outstanding names in French literary history of the last
century, published "Emily Dickinson: Poétesse et
Recluse" ["Emily Dickinson: Poètess and Recluse"]
in the prestigious Revue de Paris.[65]   At the beginning of the article, Maurois states that while
Dickinson may be inferior to Shakespeare, Shelley,
and Swinburne, she is certainly the equal of Poe
and Blake.   Maurois considers her poems difficult
and sometimes "unsuccessful" but most of them he
considers "masterpieces."   Despite a certain "morbid romanticism," Dickinson displays, above all,
a "solid, satirical, and independent" mind.   Among
other examples of Dickinson's independence,
Maurois discusses her refusal at Mount Holyoke to
fake a religious conviction.   On the other hand,
she could also be "puerile" and childish: as an
example of childishness, Maurois mentions the fact
that the men who counted in her life all were
guides for a "child" in some way--a father, a
teacher, a reverend, and a literary mentor.[66]

[63]Cf. Arnavon who did not consider Dickinson's language "sonorous"; footnote 60.

[64]André Maurois made a name in every literary genre; he was a novelist, a poet, a biogra-
pher, an essayist, and a critic.

[65]André Maurois, "Emily Dickinson: Poétesse
et Recluse," Revue de Paris, 60 (November 1954),
1-13.

[66]It is noteworthy that Maurois does not read
this pattern of Dickinson's life in a Freudian
manner; cf. Catel's discussion of the same bio-

In the latter part of the article, Maurois concentrates on the poems themselves: he sees Dickinson's "economy in language" matched by few. Horace and Blake, and, in France, Mallarmé and Valéry would be worthy competitors, in his opinion. "A queen makes up her own rules," Maurois continues. The words of her poems are those which suggested themselves to her as appropriate; often the readers can only guess at the meaning. But then, Maurois adds, she is in good company: Mallarmé and T. S. Eliot did the same. Finally, Maurois touches on the themes of Dickinsons' poetry: in his opinion, they are the same as one finds in the production of any great poet. However, Maurois considers the theme of death the one most successfully treated; it is reminiscent of Kafka in the sense that Dickinson sees a dual quality in God, attractive and frightening at the same time.[67]

Raymond Las Vergnas in 1955 published "Lettres anglo-américaines" ["Anglo-American Literature"] which was, in part, a review of Simon's collection of translated poems.[68] In Las Vergnas' opinion, Simon was successful in the formidable task of translation. Thanks to Simon, Las Vergnas continues, Dickinson now has a vastly increased French audience. Las Vergnas, in paying tribute to several literary critics, mentions in particular Arnavon and his Histoire Littéraire des États-Unis,[69] André Maurois who writes with his

---

graphical material, footnotes 4-7.

[67]Maurois, too, has translated some lines, even stanzas, and has incorporated them in his article.

[68]Raymond Las Vergnas, "Lettres anglo-américaines," Hommes et Mondes, 10 (June 1955), 450-52.

[69]Cf. footnote 59.

"customary sense of balance, elegance, and clari-
ty,"[70] and Maurice Le Breton.[71]

In 1955, André Maurois included a reprint of
his 1954 article on Dickinson in the famous Robert
et Elizabeth Browning: Portraits suivis de quelques autres [Robert and Elizabeth Browning: Portraits Followed by Some Others].[72]

A year later, Alain Bosquet published
Anthologie de la Poésie Américaine des Origines à
Nos Jours [Anthology of American Poetry from the
Beginning to the Present].[73] Although the selection
of Dickinson poems is small compared to, for instance, the selection in Simon's book, it contains
sixteen poems in Bosquet's translation.[74] In ad-

[70]Cf. footnote 65.

[71]Cf. footnote 52.

[72]André Maurois, Robert et Elizabeth Browning: Portraits suivis de quelques autres (Paris:
Bernard Grasset, 1955), pp. 45-64.

[73]Alain Bosquet, Anthologie de la Poésie
Américaine des Origines à Nos Jours (Paris:
Librairie Stock, Delamain et Boutelleau, 1956), pp.
20-21, 94-103, 285-86. Subsequent references to
this book will be cited as Anthologie. Alain
Bosquet is professor of American literature and
the author of numerous novels, collections of
poetry, as well as scholarly works on, for instance, Whitman, several recent American poets,
Ionesco, and Solzhenitsyn. In 1968, he was awarded a prestigious prize for his collected works by
l'Académie française.

[74]The translations are of complete poems and
as close to the original as can be reasonably expected. The sixteen poems are: "Je suis Personne!
Qui es-tu?" ["I am Nobody! Who are you?"]; "Le
cerveau est plus vaste que le ciel" ["The Brain--

dition to the translations, each poet is commented on by Bosquet. He does not place Dickinson within any literary tradition; according to him, she can be compared to Emily Brontë but equally well to Spinoza, or even Newton. She has written "perhaps the most disconcerting poetry that any woman has ever written." Bosquet concludes his remarks by stating that Dickinson is "one of the three or four greatest poetesses of any time period."[75]

In an issue of Études Anglaises devoted to "L'Éternel Problème de la Traduction" ["The Eternal Problem of Translation"], several critics commented on different translations into French.[76] Maurice Le Breton reviewed Jean Simon's 1954 trans-

---

is wider than the Sky"]; "Y aura-t-il pour de vrai un matin?" ["Will there really be a 'Morning'?"]; "A trois heures trente un oiseau unique" ["At Half past Three, a single Bird"]; "L'herbe a si peu de chose à faire" ["The Grass so little has to do"]; "Entre, cher Mars!" ["Dear March--Come in"]; "Pour faire une prairie" ["To make a prairie it takes a clover and one bee"]; "Comme je ne pourrais m'arrêter pour la Mort" ["Because I could not stop for Death"]; "Je vais au ciel!" ["Going to Heaven!"]; "Je ne l'ai pas encore dit au jardin" ["I hav'nt told my garden yet"]; "Ce n'était pas la mort puisque j'étais debout" ["It was not Death, for I stood up"]; "Il y a une solitude de l'espace" ["There is a solitude of space"]; "Le vent prit les choses du nord" ["The Wind took up the Northern Things"]; "Fleurir est aboutir. Qui rencontre une fleur" ["Bloom--is Result--to meet a Flower"]; "Des fleurs: eh bien! s'il est quelqu'un" ["Flowers--Well--if anybody"]; and "Il vécut une vie de guet-apens" ["He lived the Life of Ambush"].

[75]Bosquet, Anthologie, p. 21.

[76]Maurice Le Breton, "L'Éternel Problème de la Traduction," Études Anglaises, 9 (January-March 1956), 90-91.

lations of Dickinson poems. Simon gets a good
rating by Le Breton, in particular because of his
method of translation. One must always, as a
competent translator, "rival the audacity" of the
original poems, Le Breton argues, and not be in-
timidated by them. This is exactly what Simon
has done, Le Breton continues, praising in particular the fact that Simon kept "the incomparable
conciseness" of Dickinson's poetry. Nevertheless,
Le Breton concludes his remarks on the translations, Simon is no Dickinson. The last part of
the review-article is devoted to Dickinson herself. Le Breton finds that the technique of her
poetry does not have a wide range, but the "morsels of content" are so profound and, therefore,
"modern" that her poetry never ceases to attract
the reader.

Alain Bosquet in 1957 again turned to Dickinson in his Emily Dickinson.[77] In addition to
the extensive critical comments, the book contains
"selected aphorisms," selected letters, and one
hundred poems in translation. Before considering
Dickinson, Bosquet surveys the state of American
poetry around 1862 finding little merit in the
names of the day with the one exception of Whitman. Among the poets mentioned are "the vener-
able" William Cullen Bryant, "whom nobody can
reproach of anything," "a kind of Wordsworth with
less melancholy but more common sense"; the "well-
manufactured" poems of James Russell Lowell; and
"the pleasantries" of "that perfect gentleman,"
Oliver Wendell Holmes.[78] Ralph Waldo Emerson's
poetry "is nothing but laborious compositions,"
according to Bosquet.[79] But Emily Dickinson is

[77]Emily Dickinson, ed. Alain Bosquet (Paris:
P. Seghers, 1957). Subsequent references to this
book will be cited as Dickinson.

[78]Bosquet, Dickinson, p. 16.

[79]Bosquet, Dickinson, p. 17.

different: "this tight-lipped and inebriating
poetry" resembles nothing in the poetry of her
contemporaries. She has little respect for regu-
lated labor; instead, she writes by the instinct
of the visionary. Bosquet is equally impressed
with the form and the content of Dickinson's poetry. Being the first one to utilize "free verse,"
she hardly cares whether she is intelligible,
even coherent, Bosquet maintains. In fact, it is
questionable whether she distinguishes between
prose and poetry. Bosquet particularly stresses
the quality of Dickinson's "private vocabulary."
To speak of the "profound originality" of her
language is underestimating her; she is capable of
"accepting the supreme risk" of perhaps not understanding what she herself has put down on paper.
It is no wonder, Bosquet comments, that her exe-
getes and translators have succeeded as rarely as
they have. Bosquet goes on to discuss her themes,
or rather, her "one and only theme": all is fore-
boding--one does not know of what--and all is
marvel. He feels that Dickinson's success in con-
veying her moods by disregarding "useless syntax"
and "exterior . . . corrections" is how she manages to remain of universal interest. She does
not insist, she does not moralize, and she does
not raise her voice. She remains, Bosquet observes, "an enemy of oratorical hysteria and verbal romanticism."[80] Bosquet concludes his remarks: her "irrational . . . concept of the world
remains irreplaceable."[81]

Bosquet's Emily Dickinson marked the end of
the French Dickinson criticism of the fifties. In
1961, Christian Murciaux published "Emily Dickinson" in the highly regarded Cahiers du Sud.[82]

[80]Bosquet, Dickinson, p. 56.

[81]Bosquet, Dickinson, p. 58.

[82]Christian Murciaux, "Emily Dickinson,"
Cahiers du Sud, 51 (April-May 1961), 276-89.

Murciaux first gives an over-view of Dickinson's
life but also briefly mentions her relative standing among other nineteenth-century poets according to French critics: many place her on the same
level as Poe, Emerson and Whitman, and André
Maurois considers her comparable to Blake and
Shelley.[83] Murciaux pays particular tribute to
"Jean Castel who was the first Dickinsonian in
France."[84] Murciaux, as Professor Landquist in
Sweden,[85] sees a parallel to the Weltanschauung
of the German painter Albrecht Dürer in Emily
Dickinson, particularly with regard to their
views of nature. In fact, Murciaux devotes a good
part of his article to comparisons between repre-
sentatives of different art forms. Thus, the
"brilliant colors" of Dickinson's "resurrection
poems" he compares to those of Fra Angelico; the
"exhiliration" to that of Bach's concerti and
chorals; and Dickinson's boldness to the imagery
of Blake and the Metaphysical poets.[86] Murciaux
remarks that Dickinson's vision does not permit
eloquence or sonority but that her "hard and com-
pact" words are the kind that produces vertigo in
the reader. She invented a new language, Murciaux
continues, and her verbal "economy" supplied a
pattern for the American poetry that followed.
Discussing the content of Dickinson's poetry,
Murciaux admits to being particularly impressed
by the love poetry. He totally denounces Rebecca
Patterson's suggestion of lesbianism; instead, he
reflects, one may assume that in Kate Scott Anthon,
Dickinson sees "an incarnation of Henry James's
cosmopolitan travellers," something to be admired

[83]Cf. footnote 65.

[84]Murciaux uses "Castel" but must be referring
to Jean Catel whose 1925 article was called the
first on Dickinson in France; see footnote 4.

[85]Cf. chapter II, footnote 77.

[86]Murciaux, p. 283.

and perhaps envied.[87]   Murciaux concludes that
"Emily Dickinson's legacy to America is . . .
poems as passionate and pure as the psalms that
accompanied the debarkation of the first Pil-
grims."   Within the article, Murciaux has insert-
ed some poems in complete form and others only in
part, all in his own translation.[88]

In Études Anglaises, Maurice Le Breton published a review-article in 1961. The review concerns Charles Anderson's Emily Dickinson's Poetry:
Stairway of Surprise.[89] Le Breton briefly praises
Anderson and goes on to discuss Dickinson's poetry
itself. He observes that it is "the intensity
that gives . . . [the] explosive quality to her
inspiration." She has "a thirst for extremes" and
it is not surprising that her "profound metaphors"
seem to come "straight out of a magician's bag"
rather than out of any literary tradition.

In 1963, a new collection of Dickinson poems
in translation appeared. Claude Berger and Paul
Zweig translated twenty poems introduced by
Zweig.[90] Zweig remarks that we will never know

[87]Murciaux, p. 285.

[88]Some of the poems are: "Bien en sécurité
dans leurs chambres d'albâtre" ["Safe in their
Alabaster Chambers"]; "Le Paradis n'est pas plus
distant" ["Elysium is as far as to"]; "J'ai vu
le ciel lever sa tente" ["I've known a Heaven,
like a Tent"]; and "L'âme choisit sa société"
["The Soul selects her own Society"].

[89]Maurice Le Breton, rev. of Emily Dickinson's Poetry: Stairway of Surprise by Charles R.
Anderson, Études Anglaises, 14 (July-September
1961), 279.

[90]Emily Dickinson: Twenty Poems: Vingt Poèmes,
introd. Paul Zweig, trans. Claude Berger and Paul
Zweig (Paris: Minard, Lettres Modernes, 1963).

whether Dickinson wrote because she was isolated
or whether she isolated herself in order to write;
in either case, this isolation is a remarkable
background for poetry such as hers; also, the

The twenty poems are: "Épargnés et reclus dans
leurs Chambres d'Albâtre" ["Safe in their Alabaster Chambers"]; "Parfois certain Rai de
lumière" ["There's a certain Slant of light"];
"Nuits Sauvages--Nuits Sauvages!" ["Wild Nights--
Wild Nights!"]; "Une Horloge s'arrêta" ["A Clock
stopped"]; "De Bronze--et de Feu" ["Of Bronze--
and Blaze"]; "J'entendis une Mouche bourdonner--
quand je mourus" ["I heard a Fly buzz--when I
died"]; "Je mourus pour la Beauté--mais à peine"
["I died for Beauty--but was scarce"]; "Après une
grande douleur, vient un sentiment solonnel"
["After great pain, a formal feeling comes"];
"Mon titre--est divin!" ["Title divine--is mine!"];
"Comme je ne pouvais m'arrêter pour lui" ["Because I could not stop for Death"]; "Pour être
hanté--point n'est besoin d'être chambre" ["One
need not be a Chamber--to be Haunted"]; "Ma Vie
était restée--Fusil Chargé" ["My Life had stood--
a Loaded Gun"]; "Les Huiles essentielles sont ex-
traites" ["Essential Oils--are wrung"]; "Un Être
effilé dans l'Herbe" ["A narrow Fellow in the
Grass"]; "Le Désordre dans une Maison" ["The
Bustle in a House"]; "Plus loin dans l'Été que
Les Oiseaux" ["Further in Summer than the Birds"];
"Quel mystère regne dans un puits!" ["What mystery
pervades a well!"]; "Une Route d'Evanescence"
["A Route of Evanescence"]; "Heureuse la petite
Pierre" ["How happy is the little Stone"]; and
"Vint un Vent tel une Sonnerie de Cor" ["There
came a Wind like a Bugle"]. These translations
are not only linguistically closer to the original than other French translations so far but they
convey to a remarkable extent the specific quality
of Dickinson's poetry. Part of this accomplish-
ment may be due to the fact that the translators
have used Thomas Johnson's 1955 edition of the
original poetry.

111

cultural isolation of the time offered "no intellectual nourishment, other than numerous fashion-
able but sentimental publications" of mediocre
quality.[91] In this vacuum, Dickinson produced
poetry of a "sure and inspired vision," and because of this vacuum, she was forced to create
independently, both with regard to form and to
content. Finally, Zweig turns to Dickinson's
punctuation which he considers "as careful and
calculated as the punctuation of a Mallarmé." By
using punctuation as a tool, Dickinson "imposes
pace" on the reader and "breaks the stream of
certain lines in order to regroup or halt the
words." Zweig concludes his introduction by stating that, for the first time, the French reader is
offered the poetry of this "incomparable poet,"
because the translations closely follow the Johnson edition of Dickinson's poetry.

In 1964, Robert Goffin[92] published Fil
d'Ariane Pour La Poésie [An Ariadne's Thread for
Poetry].[93] It is Goffin's thesis, in his chapter
on Emily Dickinson, that Dickinson's poetry is
consciously erotic and this to an extent that
critics have either not realized or chosen to
ignore. Goffin starts his chapter by comparing
"this woman of genius," Emily Dickinson, to
Mallarmé--and from a Mallarmé specialist, this

[91]Zweig, p. 10. Zweig does not qualify this
statement.

[92]Professor Goffin is the author of more than
ten collections of poetry, nearly ten novels, several full-length critical studies treating poetry
(for instance, Rimbaud, Verlaine, and Mallarmé),
and numerous essays on subjects ranging from historical topics in literature to the history of
jazz.

[93]Robert Goffin, "Emily Dickinson," Fil
d'Ariane Pour La Poésie (Paris: A. G. Nizet, 1964),
pp. 250-66.

comparison is high praise. At the beginning of
his introduction to Dickinson, Goffin argues that
it is the linguistic originality of Dickinson that
makes her "the greatest poetess in the world."
Goffin observes that one "makes poetry" not with
ideas, but with words, as Mallarmé stated a long
time ago. Goffin continues that "she [Dickinson]
manipulates words as if they had never been used
before." In proving his point that Dickinson is,
above all, a poet of eroticism, Goffin effectively uses explication de texte, traditionally the
favorite of any French literary critic, to prove
his thesis. He primarily builds his argument
around the poem "I like to see it lap the Miles."
Goffin admits that, certainly, this poem can be
seen as prompted by the inauguration of train
service between Amherst and Belchertown. But,
Goffin argues, one has to go further than American
critics have done "with their customary prudish-
ness." The reading of this poem that first comes
to mind is explicitly sexual, Goffin continues.[94]

[94]Goffin does not mention Wallace Stevens in
particular, although several of his poems invite
sexual readings. Goffin's reading of this particular poem, "I like to see it lap the Miles," is a
parallel to a sexual interpretation of Wallace
Stevens' "The Emperor of Ice Cream," although, of
the two, the Dickinson poem lends itself more obviously to such a reading. Another Stevens poem
which invites comparisons with Dickinson is, for
instance, "To the One of Fictive Music," and the
use of words such as "queen," "diviner love,"
"fragrant mothers," in comparison to the "emperor"
of ice cream and Dickinson's use of royal titles.
Goffin might have further strengthened his case
by adding an explication of, for example, "Title
divine--is mine!" which seems to be a perfect companion piece to "I like to see it lap the Miles."
Many other Dickinson poems might lend themselves
to similar readings; numbers 517; 1092; 1720;
1721; 1722; 1729; and 1732, among others (the
numbering is from the Johnson edition). Cf.

He goes on to say that "she sings of what cannot
be clearly expressed. She speaks without revealing, paraphrases the effect without mentioning
the cause." In the latter part of the chapter,
Goffin offers brief explications of other Dickinson poems which he reads in the same vein, such
as "Mine--by the Right of the White Election!,"
where Goffin disagrees with Charles Anderson's
religious reading. Among other poems considered
in this light are "My Life had Stood--a Loaded
Gun" and "Because I could not stop for Death."
Goffin considers the latter poem a particularly
good proof for his thesis, specifically on account of the "horse" and "ride" imagery. Goffin
affirms: "I humbly suggest that the poetess em-
ploys biblical or religious language . . . to
suggest her sensual trance . . . [using] parallels
that swell to the point of eroticism."

My review of research through 1977 indicates
that only one doctoral dissertation has been written in France on Emily Dickinson. In 1964, Marie
Elsa Copeland wrote "Le Créateur et la création
dans la poésie de Jules Supervielle et d'Emily
Dickinson" ["The Creator and the Creation in the
Poetry of Jules Supervielle and Emily Dickinson"].95 Copeland first states that these two
poets are much underrated. Dickinson was a recluse; Supervielle was a sophisticated, inter-
nationally oriented individual. They may seem to
have little in common; yet, Copeland argues, that
is not so. For example, Copeland finds that they
both had a need for solitude and seem to have
thrived on it artistically.96 The novelty of

Cestre's comments on "Nuits éperdues! nuits
éperdues!," p. 99 of this chapter.

95Marie Elsa Copeland, "Le Créateur et la
création dans la poésie de Jules Supervielle et
d'Emily Dickinson," Diss. University of Paris 1964.

96Cf. Emil Staiger, chapter II, footnote 100.

their respective styles Copeland views as another common interest. Copeland's discussion of Dickinson's imagery predictably deals with mountains, the night, noon, and, above all, the sea, which is similarly treated by Dickinson and Supervielle, according to Copeland. Copeland's explication of the symbolism of the sea comes close to the discussions of Blom and Inder Nath Kher, respectively.[97] In discussion the word "heart" in the works of both poets, Copeland observes that for Supervielle, the heart is all that counts in life, whereas in Dickinson's poetry, the heart "resembles a cemetery." The greatness of Dickinson's poetry, Copeland argues, does not come from the "heart," but rather the brain. She is, above all, an intellectual poet. Generally, the same physical phenomena interest the two poets and those phenomena are eventually used as metaphors. Of all the interests linking Dickinson and Supervielle, Copeland finds death to be the foremost and feels that it is perhaps as poets concerned with death that one should consider them first-rate. They both treat death in everyday terms, "to make it less frightening," Copeland suggests. Additionally, in Dickinson's art, immortality and human love are interchangeable.[98] Copeland concludes: "Both of these poets draw on the exterior universe to illustrate and explain the richness of inner life."

In 1966, Pierre Brunel published some brief comments on a poem by Paul Claudel.[99] Brunel believes that the Dickinson poem that inspired

[97]Cf. chapter III, footnotes 34-37.

[98]Cf. Goffin's reading of Dickinson's religious language as a metaphor for sensuality and sexuality.

[99]Pierre Brunel, "Le Corbeau (à propos de la transposition par Claudel d'un poème d'Emily Dickinson)," Revue des Lettres Modernes, 134-36 (1966), 113-18.

Claudel was "Water, is taught by thirst." Brunel
observes that the common denominator is "the system of correspondences . . . [and] contrasts."[100]
The Dickinson poem observes that if one has not
known thirst, one does not appreciate water; if
one has not seen the blackness of a bird, one
does not know that snow is white. Brunel goes on
to say that Claudel has "inverted" Dickinson's
poem: in the French poem, the individual needs
water to be able to recognize thirst; similarly,
the snow needs a crow to show off its whiteness.
Brunel is more concerned with the poetry of
Claudel than with that of Dickinson but acknowledges the donnée of Dickinson that is to be found
in a whole series of Claudel poems.

An important article was the last French
item to be published on Emily Dickinson in the
sixties. The title is "Emily Dickinson: une
aventure poétique" ["Emily Dickinson: A Poetic
Adventure"].[101] J. Normand first discusses the
word "adventure," defining it as "fertile disorder, as opposed to sterile order." Inventions
are born out of tortured reality, Normand suggests, and so is Emily Dickinson's poetry. Had
her life been different in its outer aspects,
Dickinson would never have made the journey "from
without to within," from reality to imagination.
Normand compares Dickinson to Pasternak and
Baudelaire: to all of them, the discovery of poetry was synonymous with the discovery of the self.
It is Normand's opinion, as it was Goffin's, that
sexuality is the core of much of Emily Dickinson's
poetry. Normand's first example is "Il est divin
mon titre" ["Title divine--is mine"]. Without the
physical imprint of sexuality and sensuality,
society would produce neither poetry nor goodness
in its highest manifestations, Normand continues,

[100]Brunel, p. 115.

[101]J. Normand, "Emily Dickinson: une aventure
poétique," Études Anglaises, 21 (1968), 152-59.

and he quotes D. H. Lawrence who said that even the rainbow has a body. The discovery of "total reality" is "carnal" in quality, Normand argues; this is how poets are born. "I am a poet. Therefore I exist," Normand concludes. These, then, are the major ingredients in Dickinson's poetry, according to Normand: the "adventure," i.e., the "fertile disorder" and the "carnal inspiration" often inseparable from so-called Metaphysical poetry, as in the cases of Dante and Donne. Normand also includes partial translations of several Dickinson poems.[102]

In 1970, a major work on Emily Dickinson was published by Guy Jean Forgue.[103] The book is called Emily Dickinson: Poèmes [Emily Dickinson: Poems].[104] It contains both critical commentary and a great number of complete poems in translation. Professor Forgue offers a thoughtful and balanced view of Dickinson's poetry. He defines her poetry as "a restless . . . meeting between fantasy and a metaphysical postulation."[105]

[102]The poems translated in part are: "Grande folie est divine sagesse" ["Much Madness is divinest Sense"]; "C'est un Dieu bien jaloux que Dieu" ["God is indeed a jealous God"]; "Étroit domain est le cercueil" ["A Coffin--is a small Domain"]; "Fais-moi un portrait du soleil" ["Make me a picture of the sun"]; "Je ne peux vivre avec toi" ["I cannot live with You"]; "Une fosse--mais le ciel pardessus" ["A Pit--but Heaven over it"]; "Comme si c'était la mer" ["As if the Sea should part"]; and "Poète était celui-là--il" ["This was a Poet-- It is That"].

[103]Guy Jean Forgue is professor at the Sorbonne.

[104]Guy Jean Forgue, Emily Dickinson: Poèmes (Aubier: Aubier-Flammarion, 1970).

[105]Forgue, p. 18.

It is "the metaphysical problems" which are the
core of Dickinson's poetry, Forgue argues. He
sees her as close to Poe in her "obsession with
death and funerals" and also to Hawthorne and
Melville. "The painful meandering of this soul
represents a modern version of Pilgrim's Prog-
ress," Forgue observes. Dickinson over-reacted
to emotions such as love and fear of death. As
in the case of Baudelaire, her mind is "a divided
kingdom" with two monarchs engaged in a dialogue.
Love is the instrument that permits her to conquer the eternal light, as in the poetry of
Marvell or Donne, Forgue observes.[106] Dickinson
uses her poetry to survive her horror of death
and her "metaphysical uncertainty"; with this
horror of death goes "a curious fascination"
which, according to Forgue, is more metaphysical
in quality than morbid or neurotic, as some critics have interpreted it.[107] Finally, Forgue
turns to the style of Dickinson's poetry, finding
its "almost brutal laconism" typical of the New
Englander in general. Forgue comments that it is
the intensity that saves Dickinson's style from
"dryness." Her poetry lives in dissonances and
surprises; in this, he finds her reminiscent of
T. S. Eliot, Wallace Stevens, Marianne Moore, or
Robert Lowell. Forgue also suggests ties with
Ezra Pound, William Carlos Williams, and e. e.
cummings. The latter part of Professor Forgue's
book contains his translations.[108]

[106]Forgue notes that "love," innocent as it
may be, often approaches an "erotic dream" (p.
29), a viewpoint close to those of Normand and
Goffin.

[107]Cf. chapter II, footnote 131.

[108]Some of the poems are: "En lieu sûr dans
leur chambre d'albâtre" ["Safe in their Alabaster
Chambers"]; "Embrasement d'or" ["Blazing in Gold
and quenching in Purple"]; "Il est certain biais
de lumière" ["There's a certain Slant of light"];

The last item of the seventies to be discussed here is John Brown's Panorama de La Littérature Contemporaine Aux États-Unis [Panorama of Contemporary Literature in the United States].[109] Brown mentions her only briefly but groups her with "some exceptions of genius--Walt Whitman, Emily Dickinson, Edgar Allan Poe, [and] Emerson." Generally, Brown finds American poetry "a pale imitation of English poetry."[110]

Finally to be considered are three reference works, the first one from 1956. Régis Michaud has contributed the small entry on Dickinson in Laffont-Bompiani's Dictionnaire biographique des

---

"Bronze embrasé" ["Of Bronze--and Blaze"]; "L'âme choisit sa compagnie" ["The Soul selects her own Society"]; "Il vint un jour au coeur de l'été" ["There came a Day at Summer's full"]; "Voici ma missive au monde" ["This is my letter to the World"]; "C'était un Poète--Celui" ["This was a Poet--It is That"]; "J'étais mort pour le Beau, mais à peine" ["I died for Beauty--but was scarce"]; "Doux abri des maisons" ["Sweet--safe-- Houses"]; "Ce n'était pas la mort, car j'étais debout" ["It was not Death, for I stood up"]; "Pour être hanté nul besoin n'est de chambre" ["One need not be a Chamber--to be Haunted"]; "Le tonnerre le plus lointain que j'entendis" ["The farthest Thunder that I heard"]; "De Dieu nous sollicitons" ["Of God we ask one favor"]; "Lorsqu'on met le départ à l'encan" ["The Auctioneer of Parting"]; "Sans paraître étonner" ["Apparently with no surprise"]; and "La Beauté m'étouffe à mourir" ["Beauty crowds me till I die"]; Forgue's translations are unquestionably the most successful so far in French (1977).

[109]John Brown, Panorama de La Littérature Contemporaine Aux États-Unis (1954; rpt. Paris: Librairie Gallimard, 1971), pp. 49, 274.

[110]Brown, p. 274.

119

auteurs [Biographical Dictionary of Writers].[111]
In addition to the biographical information, some
of the best known sentences written by Michaud on
Dickinson are quoted: "Emily's poetry exudes an
odor of prison but is illuminated by thought . . . .
A whole school of poets will recognize itself in
this laconism."[112] Among the few bibliographical
entries is Whicher's book on Dickinson.

The second reference book is the most famous
in France, commonly referred to as Larousse.[113]
Dickinson, together with Poe and Whitman, "domi-
nates" nineteenth-century American poetry, the
anonymous writer observes, but adds that her poet-
ty is "of uneven quality." With Dickinson, poetry
was "an act of faith"; her whole life she devoted
"passionately and exclusively" to poetry. Larousse
gives no bibliographical information.

In 1973, another Larousse contained consider-
ably more information on Emily Dickinson.[114] The
writer observes that despite her religious skepticism and inner revolt, Emily Dickinson could not
avoid the imprint of the Puritan milieu; therefore, death is her favorite topic. One can also
"compare [her] . . . to an Elizabeth Barrett without a Browning." Fundamentally, the author observes, Dickinson is a Metaphysical poet with two

[111]Régis Michaud, "Emily Dickinson,"
Dictionnaire biographique des auteurs (Paris:
S.E.D.E. et V. Bompiani, 1956), I, 422-23. Sub-
sequent references to this book will be cited as
Dictionnaire.

[112]Dictionnaire, p. 423.

[113]"Dickinson (Emily)," Grand Larousse
encyclopédique (Paris: Librairie Larousse, 1961),
IV, 65.

[114]J. C. [signature], "Dickinson (Emily),"
La Grande Encyclopédie (Paris: Librairie
Larousse, 1973), VII, 3845.

favorite subjects, death and love. Thus, her subject matter is not novel but her style is; "this
nervous style is itself a kind of metaphor for the
difficulty of living." At the end of the article,
Dickinson is compared to Allen Tate, Marianne
Moore, Robert Lowell, T. S. Eliot, and Hart Crane,
but, concludes the writer, "one would over-esti-
mate this crisp work [Dickinson's poetry] in comparing it to that of Walt Whitman." In the bibliographical information, Whicher, Chase, Anderson, Leyda, and Gelpi are mentioned.

Only one major work on Emily Dickinson has
been published in French-speaking Switzerland. In
1945, Félix Ansermoz-Dubois published Emily Dickinson: Choix de Poèmes [Emily Dickinson: Selected
Poems].115 About half of the book is devoted to
translated poems. As the first major collection
of Dickinson poems in French and as a source of
inspiration for many such collections to come
within France proper, the work might have been
incorporated into the general French material.
However, it deserves its own place for several
reasons. It is noteworthy, for instance, that
the always culturally sensitive and in many fields
pioneering little nation of Switzerland sensed the
need for a substantial collection of translated
Emily Dickinson poetry as early as 1945. It is
true that Ansermoz-Dubois' translations have been
denounced by several French critics--many of them
competitors in the field of Dickinson translations
--and also that these translations may not measure
up to the outstanding level of, for instance,
those of Guy Jean Forgue. Still, Ansermoz-Dubois
remains a pioneer; in Josephine Pollitt's words,
"Dickinson assumes her full stature across the
seas," thanks to Professor Ansermoz-Dubois.116
Pollitt pays tribute to Jean Catel and the pres-

115Félix Ansermoz-Dubois, Emily Dickinson:
Choix de Poèmes (Genève: Éditions du Continent,
1945).

116Josephine Pollitt, "In Lands I Never Saw,"

tigious Revue des Deux Mondes but Ansermoz-Dubois
gets most of her attention. Pollitt concludes
her article by observing that "it is a happy
matter to have the perspective of a European
scholar, an enthusiast of Emily's own spirit."[117]
She also quotes, "Je ne suis rien," Ansermoz-
Dubois' translation of "I'm Nobody! Who are you?".
In "Emily beyond the Alps," Pollitt reviewed Professor Ansermoz-Dubois' work.[118] In discussing
"the first book in French devoted altogether to
this American poet [Dickinson]," Pollitt comments,
referring to Dickinson's own use of French words,
that the French language "at times seems actually
to release something imprisoned in the 'curious
hermetism' of her work." About the actual quality
of Ansermoz-Dubois' translations, Pollitt cautiously observes: "Unlike his predecessors in
French, this translator is ambitious to keep as
close as possible to the original. . . . For those
who favor a freer translation, the work of M.
Ansermoz-Dubois affords a wonderfully heady dis-
pute."

In his critical commentary, Professor
Ansermoz-Dubois observes that, apart from Whitman,
no other has so influenced the American poetry of
the preceding thirty years (i.e., before 1945) as
Dickinson. Her "disconcerting" imagination together with her "audacity" in linguistic matters
is a continuing source of inspiration. Ansermoz-
Dubois deplores the fact that so few major French-
speaking critics have devoted time to "this great

Guests in Eden, ed. Alma G. Watson (New York: Zeta
Chapter Phi Delta Gamma, 1946), pp. 34-37. Subse-
quent references to this article will be cited as
"Lands."

[117]Pollitt, "Lands," p. 37.

[118]Josephine Pollitt, "Emily beyond the Alps,"
Saturday Review, 29 (April 6, 1946), 20.

artist."[119] According to Ansermoz-Dubois, Dickinson's artistry is even more obvious in her prose than in her poetry. The themes of her poetry, Ansermoz-Dubois observes, are only three: love and death, but, above all, nature. He concludes his comments by stating that, in all probability, Dickinson's poetry has "the highest voltage of all Anglo-Saxon poetry."

Summary of French Criticism of Emily Dickinson

        In looking back over this review of French Dickinson criticism, one finds that the first appearance of Emily Dickinson's name in a scholarly context in France occurred in 1925. Of the countries surveyed in this study, France was the first to recognize the importance of Emily Dickinson's poetry (with the exception of two German articles of 1898). This fact is not surprising: France has traditionally shown a strong interest in poetry, in the woman-artist, and in the psychology involved in both the artistic creation and its creator. Significantly, Professor Jean Catel's article of 1925 (see footnote 4) is written by a noted scholar of American literature; it concentrates on the psychology of the artist--a woman--and it is highly appreciative. Two of the four articles (one part of a book) that appeared in France during the twenties were written by Catel. In the second (see footnote 8), Catel views Dickinson in a somewhat more critical light: he still admires her sophisticated intellectuality, but, at the same time, considers her "cold to the touch." The third publication of the twenties came from Professor Régis Michaud, by far the most renowned French specialist of English literature at the time (see footnote 15). "A whole school of poets will recognize itself in this laconism" is a sen-

[119]Among those few, he mentions Catel, Feuillerat, and Leyris.

tence often quoted from Michaud's comments on
Dickinson. On the whole, Michaud is highly appreciative of the simple, "naked" quality of her
poetry as opposed to the romanticism of her American predecessors. Albert Feuillerat ended the
decade with "La Vie Secrète d'Une Puritaine" (see
footnote 18). As the title suggests, the major
part of the article is devoted to the psychological implications of Puritan upbringing. Like
Michaud, Feuillerat stresses the "nude" and passionate side of Dickinson's poetry and regards
this "indiscreet" poetry as an attempt to escape
Puritanism. Feuillerat has the highest praise
for the content of Dickinson's poetry but little
for the form of it.

Jean Catel dominated Dickinson criticism during the thirties. Out of six items, five articles
and a chapter of a book, three were written by
Catel. Professor Léon Bocquet wrote "La Littérature
Américaine," a devastating critique of American
literature in general (see footnote 22). Bocquet
makes one of his rare exceptions, offering nothing
but praise, for the "sincere and profound work" of
Dickinson. John Jacoby published a book in 1931
and in the chapter devoted to Dickinson, considers
her exclusively a mystic, mainly a "nature mystic,"
in line with the thesis of his Mysticisme dans la
Pensée Américaine (see footnote 26). Only Dickinson's poems about nature show her "within the absolute power of inspiration," according to Jacoby.
Catel, in an article mainly treating Whitman, again
pays tribute to Dickinson's "instinct for poetry"
and stresses his opinion that she is equal to Whitman (see footnote 30). In his next article, published in 1933 and devoted exclusively to Dickinson, Catel, as the first in France, attempts to
categorize Dickinson's poetry according to themes
(see footnote 32). The end of the article implies
Catel's preference for Dickinson over Whitman. In
1935, Catel wrote his third article on Dickinson
during this decade, this one starting out as a discussion of Pollitt's and Taggard's books on the
poet (see footnote 34). In this article, Catel

questions the value of biographical information as
a means to the interpretation of art. Pierre
Leyris' "Poèmes et Lettres d'Emily Dickinson" was
the last publication of the thirties, the first to
contain complete translations of Dickinson poems
(see footnote 37). Leyris stresses Dickinson's
ties with the Metaphysical poets.

The five items published in the forties were
all part of full-length books. Jean Catel was the
first to publish on Dickinson in the twenties; the
first publication of the forties was also his (see
footnote 39). This book of translations of American poetry includes six poems by Dickinson. In
the same year, Professor Charles Cestre published
La Littérature Américaine (see footnote 41).
Cestre attributes to Dickinson "the gift of a genius" and sees her, together with William Vaughn
Moody, as the great precursor of modern American
poetry. He is particularly appreciative of the
open sensuality of her love poems, an opinion
wholeheartedly shared by Robert Goffin later on.
As the first in France, Cestre finds the form of
Dickinson's poetry impeccable: she "sacrifices
the finished form to the suggestive form." Similar praise for the linguistic ability of Dickinson came from Léonie Villard in her La Poésie
Américaine (see footnote 45). In addition to this
praise, Villard points out as noteworthy the fact
that it is a woman poet who offers "the supreme
manifestation of a world vision." In 1948, Professor Cestre published another book on American
literature, this one exclusively on poetry (see
footnote 48). Cestre repeats his opinion that it
is Dickinson's linguistic originality that is her
particular strength. As before, he admires her
for forgetting "the prudence of the Puritan moral
code" in her love poetry. Maurice Le Breton, in
his Anthologie de la Poésie Américaine Contemporaine,
classified Dickinson as an Imagist (see footnote
52). Like Cestre and Villard, Le Breton considers
the linguistic novelty the most outstanding and
durable quality of Dickinson's poetry.

125

As in Sweden, the fifties saw a marked increase in Dickinson criticism in France. Ten
items were published: two were books on Emily
Dickinson; four were parts of full-length books;
and four were articles (one a reprint). Jacques-
Fernand Cahen comes close to Le Breton in seeing
Dickinson as a precursor of the Imagists (see
footnote 56). Cahen admires Dickinson's language
rather than her themes which he considers "far
from new." Professor Cyrille Arnavon, in his
Histoire Littéraire des États-Unis, also places
Dickinson in the tradition of the Metaphysical
poets, praising her "nude" language and disregard
for conventional taste (see footnote 59). 1954
was a landmark in Dickinson publications because
it saw the first full-length book of translated
Dickinson poetry (see footnote 62). Professor
Jean Simon, the author and translator, sees a
definite difference in quality between Dickinson's
themes, called "elementary" and "conventional,"
and her handling of language, considered "the
life of her poems." The same year, André Maurois
argued along the same lines: he suggests that in
linguistic sophistication, Dickinson is matched
by few, perhaps only by poets such as Horace,
Blake and Valéry (see footnote 65). Maurois, too,
finds her themes of less interest. The theme of
death, however, he considers successfully treated
and thus ends his now famous essay. In 1956,
another collection of translations with critical
commentary appeared--Alain Bosquet's Anthologie
de la Poésie Américaine des Origines à Nos Jours
(see footnote 73). The ordinarily harshly critical Bosquet considers Dickinson "one of the three
or four greatest poetesses of any time period."
Bosquet does not comment specifically on the language; rather, he considers Dickinson's mind comparable to those of Spinoza and Newton. Maurice
Le Breton, in discussing the dangers of translations in general and Simon's Dickinson translations in particular, gives a high rating to
Simon's linguistic "audacity," although to expect
anybody to be quite as good as Dickinson would be
unreasonable, observes Le Breton (see footnote 76).

126

In Dickinson's poetry, Le Breton praises "the morsels of content" more than the novelty of the language. Alain Bosquet was the last in this decade to publish on Dickinson (see footnote 77). The critical Bosquet is unimpressed with most American poetry before Dickinson; in her poetry, he considers content and language of equally high standard, "irreplaceable."

In the sixties, seven items were published on Emily Dickinson, one book, one chapter of a book, four articles, and one doctoral dissertation. In 1961, Christian Murciaux published "Emily Dickinson" (see footnote 82). Murciaux, like Professor Landquist in Sweden, sees parallels between Dickinson and Albrecht Dürer. All through the article, he points out parallels between Dickinson on one hand, and composers, painters, as well as other poets, on the other hand. Murciaux rates Dickinson's love poetry high, but, generally, he considers the strength of her poetry to be the use of language. Maurice Le Breton, again in the review of a book, sees in Dickinson's poetry too much novelty and originality for it to be associated with any literary tradition; rather, it seems to come "straight out of a magician's bag" (see footnote 89). The "sure and inspired vision" of an "incomparable poet" is praised by Berger and Zweig in their 1963 collection of Dickinson translations (see footnote 90). In 1964, Robert Goffin devotes a chapter of a book to "the greatest poetess in the world" (see footnote 93). Goffin argues that Dickinson's poetry is primarily erotic, and very consciously so. Consequently, his is not a Freudian reading; he merely regards her major theme to be sexuality and this in a more explicit and, therefore, "modern" way than critics in general have dared see it. In her dissertation of the same year, Marie Elsa Copeland compared Dickinson to the modern French poet, Jules Supervielle (see footnote 95). She sees Dickinson as an intellectual poet, primarily concerned with death; as a death poet, she is called first-rate. Copeland suggests that immortality and human love are

127

interchangeable as themes in Dickinson's poetry, and here she comes close to Goffin. In an article of 1966, Pierre Brunel argued that the donnée of many poems by the famous Paul Claudel comes from Emily Dickinson (see footnote 99). In his tight argument, Brunel offers an explication de texte of Dickinson's "Water, is taught by thirst." J. Normand published an article that comes very close to Goffin's thesis that sexuality is the core of Dickinson's poetry (see footnote 101). Without sexuality, society would produce neither poetry nor generosity and compassion in human beings, Normand suggests.

Out of two publications of the seventies, Guy Jean Forgue's Emily Dickinson: Poèmes was a major one (see footnote 104). Forgue covers both content and style. He sees death--in Dickinson, a concern more metaphysical than neurotic in quality --and love--by Forgue regarded as intensely erotic along the lines indicated by Goffin and Normand-- as the two major themes of Dickinson's poetry. He suggests that the "intensity" and "the dissonances and surprises" save her style from "dryness." She is in good company in this respect, Forgue comments; he compares her to, among others, T. S. Eliot.

The other book, John Brown's Panorama de la Littérature Contemporaine Aux États-Unis, devotes relatively little space to Dickinson (see footnote 109). However, the comments are extremely complimentary; Brown groups Dickinson with "some exceptions [i.e., in American literature] of genius."

Within the French criticism on Emily Dickinson, there are some important common denominators. First of all, there is virtually no dissenting voice in the general acclaim of the poet. There is no traceable increase or decrease in the appreciation of the artist. Even as early as 1925, it was Jean Catel's opinion, stated in his first article, that Dickinson's poetry had never been appreciated to the extent that it deserved.

Although French critics may disagree over the relative merits of form versus content, an overwhelming majority of them are especially impressed with the language of the poet. It is as a stylist that she is most often called first-rate, or even, in Goffin's words, "the greatest poetess in the world." This intense interest in style is, of course, not surprising in a nation that cherishes its classical heritage and has had a preoccupation with linguistic considerations since Roman times.

Another common denominator is the tendency of a great many critics to translate the poetry, even though the translator may not be primarily a poet, but a critic. In the vast majority of French publications on Emily Dickinson, at least parts of poems are offered in translation.

So the critical reputation of Emily Dickinson in one of the two major continental countries in Europe, France, is a relatively homogeneous one in its solid appreciation of the poet. The other major country, Germany, is of a distinctly different critical temperament. Emily Dickinson and Germany will be the subject of the next chapter.

V.   Germany

Anyone making the statement that American
fiction and drama have appealed more to the Germans than American poetry has is likely to be told
that such a statement is subjective or, at least,
a minor curiosity in view of both the quantity and
quality of the poetry that Germany itself has produced. But there is evidence to support the statement. In Hans Galinsky's[1] words, "books about
American poets, with the exception of Whitman,
Pound, and Eliot, are rare here . . . [and] substantial studies devoted particularly to Emily
Dickinson or William Carlos Williams . . . even
rarer." Galinsky goes on to say: "The German interest in the American novel, short story, and
drama is inversely proportional to the interest in
[American] poetry."[2]

[1]Hans Galinsky, together with Klaus Lubbers,
may be the best known Anglicist of Germany. Hans
Galinsky is professor at Universität Mainz and
among his numerous publications are the following:
Der Lucretia Stoff in der Weltliteratur [The
Lucretia Material in World Literature]; Die Fami-
lie in Drama von Thomas Heywood [The Family in the
Drama of Thomas Heywood]; Die Sprache des Ameri-
kaners [The Language of the American]; Deutschland
in der Sicht von D. H. Lawrence und T. S. Eliot
[Germany as Seen by D. H. Lawrence and T. S.
Eliot]; and Sprache und Sprachkunstwerk in Amerika
[Language and Linguistic Art in America].

[2]Hans Galinsky, Wegbereiter Moderner Ameri-
kanischer Lyrik: Interpretations- und Rezeptions-
studien zu Emily Dickinson und William Carlos
Williams [Pathfinders in Modern American Poetry:
Studies in the Interpretation and Reception of
Emily Dickinson and William Carlos Williams]
(Heidelberg: Carl Winter Universitätsverlag, 1968),
p. 5. Galinsky also cites statistics of transla-

The first mention of Emily Dickinson in the
German language also happened to be the first mention of her in any foreign tongue. The article,
in two parts, was published in a German newspaper
in Chicago and written by a German-American, A. E.
[signature].3 As is often the case in French critical material, A. E. also offers Dickinson poems
in translation; of the four translated poems, two
are complete and two are partial.4 A. E. comments
more on the letters than on the poems of Dickinson.
Generally, this early view of the work of Emily
Dickinson is close to opinions voiced in recent
decades. A. E. suggests that American life with
its "instinct for conventional leveling" is not
conducive to great achievements: "outstanding individuals find themselves forced into the stream
of some popular trend and assume the color [of
that trend] without knowing or wanting to." A. E.
goes on to say that only three American poets
managed to save themselves by retreating to "an
island"--Thoreau, Whitman, and Emily Dickinson.
A. E. calls her talent "one of genius," philosoph-
ically oriented, and sees her as realizing "the
lack of importance of conventional undertakings."
A. E. considers her letters important literature;
he discusses in particular a letter about Jenny

---

tions, theater season offerings, and so on, to
back up his statement. Subsequent references to
this book will be cited as Wegbereiter.

3A. E. [signature], "Emily Dickinson," Der
Westen [Chicago], June 12, 1898, Sec. 3, p. 1, and
June 19, 1898, Sec. 3, p. 1.

4The poems are: "Es dünkt der Wahn ein gött-
lich Sinn" ["Much Madness is divinest Sense"];
"Erst fordert Lust das Herz" ["The Heart asks
Pleasure--first"]; "Könnt ich ein Herz am brechen
hindern" ["If I can stop one Heart from breaking"];
and "Die Seele wählt die Freunde sich" ["The Soul
selects her own Society"].

Lind,[5] finding that it was not so much her singing
as her personality and foreign accent (i.e., the
unexpected) that appealed to Emily Dickinson.

A. E.'s article is also the first to compare
Dickinson to the German poetess Annette von
Droste-Hülshoff, a comparison that has since become a commonplace in German criticism. A. E.
comments that "they [the two poetesses] do not
sacrifice the thought to the form," but regard
form and content as one to an extent that was rare
at the time. It is A. E.'s opinion that Dickinson's greatness is that she "sang . . . because
she had to," disregarding the conventional rules
of poetry and the possibility of being misunder-
stood because of this disregard for conventional
form. As for the content, A. E. considers the
love poetry superior; in his esteem for both Dickinson's style and her poems treating love, A. E.
comes close to a French appreciation.

This article by a German-American apparently
did little to stimulate interest from Germany.
Helmut Papajewski points out that "many public
libraries were . . . in a deplorable state and
. . . printing facilities in Germany up to 1949
were insufficient."[6] These facts, in addition to
political unrest and the pressure of two lost wars

[5]The Swedish singer whose statue stands in
Battery Park on the southernmost tip of Manhattan,
New York. A. E. does not identify the specific
letter or quote from it. See Mabel Loomis Todd,
ed., Letters of Emily Dickinson (Cleveland: World
Publishing Company, 1951) and Thomas H. Johnson,
ed., Letters of Emily Dickinson (Cambridge, Mass.:
Harvard University Press, 1958).

[6]Helmut Papajewski, "The Critical Reception
of Hemingway's Works in Germany since 1920," The
Literary Reputation of Hemingway in Europe, ed.
Roger Asselineau (New York: New York University
Press, 1965), p. 77.

133

did little to encourage literary criticism. Among the trickling of publications on Dickinson before the end of World War II, there was <u>Die Englische Literatur von der Renaissance bis zur Aufklärung</u> [English Literature from the Renaissance to the Enlightenment].[7] Emily Dickinson is mentioned briefly: she, together with Walt Whitman, is said to be the perfect example of transcendentalism. Even though this statement might be questioned, the next one would not: Dickinson's influence on "modern" poets is called "immense." The authors compare Dickinson to Blake, a comparison considered valid by many critics to this day. Discussing the content of Dickinson's poetry in general, the authors remark that the poetess is "puritanically shy," an opinion not shared by most European critics, certainly not the French.

A reference to Dickinson was made in 1928 by <u>Internationale Zeitschrift für Individualpsychologie</u>.[8] Without comments, Dickinson's poem "Each Life Converges to some Centre" precedes an article entitled "Elternsünden" ["The Sins of Parents"]. The author of the article discusses the "sin" of regarding one's child as "property" without realizing that every new individual is unique and will have to find its own life path. Evidently, the psychologist-author considered the Dickinson poem, in its original English version, the best introduction to the article.

Still another German-American, Friedrich

[7]Wolfgang Keller and Bernard Fehr, <u>Die Englische Literatur von der Renaissance bis zur Aufklärung</u> (Wildpark-Potsdam: Akademische Verlagsgesellschaft Athenaion M. B. H., 1928), p. 84.

[8]<u>Internationale Zeitschrift für Individualpsychologie</u>, 6 (September-October 1928), 386. This magazine is a professional publication for psychologists where literary material would not

Bruns, published Die Amerikanische Dichtung der
Gegenwart [American Contemporary Poetry] in 1930.[9]
Bruns explains that Dickinson and Stephen Crane
are included because, for all practical purposes,
they have to be considered contemporary. Bruns
calls Dickinson a poet of the small things in life
but, at the same time, a "visionary," a realist
who shies away from worn-out metaphors. Thus, he
sees Dickinson as a perfect parallel to Droste-
Hülshoff, just as A. E. had done already in 1898.
Bruns has reservations regarding Dickinson's
language; her technique often seems "naive" and
"unskilled." But, he adds, the rhythm is perfect
for her message and there is "something natural
about her expression" that always is "the sign of
genius." Bruns quotes four poems by Dickinson,
in English, since, according to him, poetry does
not lend itself to translation.[10]

In the avante-garde Europäische Revue, Hans
Hennecke published a brief article "Emily Dickinson: Gedichte" ["Emily Dickinson: Poems"] in
1937.[11] Hennecke calls Dickinson "the most outstanding genius in North-American poetry," together with Whitman, perhaps the finest poetess since
Sappho. Hennecke, above all, praises the language;
he, too, compares Dickinson to Droste-Hülshoff,

---

ordinarily be found.

[9]Friedrich Bruns, Die Amerikanische Dichtung
der Gegenwart (Leipzig und Berlin: Verlag B. G.
Teubner, 1930), pp. 1, 73-74.

[10]The four poems are: "To my quick ear the
Leaves--conferred"; "I felt a Funeral, in my Brain";
"If I should'nt be alive"; and "My life closed
twice before its close."

[11]Hans Hennecke, "Emily Dickinson: Gedichte,"
Europäische Revue, 8 (April 1937), 297-301.

particularly with regard to the "unbelievable precision" of the metaphors where intellect and heart
have become one. There follow three complete
Dickinson poems in Hennecke's translation.[12]

Right after the end of World War II, Walter
F. Schirmer published Kurze Geschichte der
Englischen Literatur: Von den Anfängen bis zur
Gegenwart [Brief History of the English Literature:
From the Beginnings to the Present].[13] His comments on Dickinson are indeed brief but appreciative. He stresses her position as a pioneer in
the field of poetry; even though her technique may
seem undeveloped, there is such a oneness in
thought and presentation that even her paradoxes
add to the reader's understanding. Her poetry is
closely related to the Metaphysical poets,
Schirmer comments, just as American poetry of this
century is related to hers. Of her different
categories of poems, Schirmer seems to prefer her
love poetry.[14]

[12]The three poems are: "Dem ich mich nie
gestellt, der Tod" ["Because I could not stop for
Death"]; "Ich koste Tränke, nie gebraut" ["I taste
a liquor never brewed"]; and "In das Dunkel meiner
Not" ["On the Bleakness of my Lot"].

[13]Walter F. Schirmer, Kurze Geschichte der
Englischen Literatur: Von den Anfängen bis zur
Gegenwart (Halle-Saale: Max Niemeyer Verlag, 1945),
p. 228.

[14]Strictly speaking, an Austrian was the
first to write on Emily Dickinson in German in the
forties: Elizabeth Granichstaedten-Czerva, "Bildersprache bei Emily Dickinson" ["Imagery in Emily
Dickinson"], Diss. University of Vienna 1940.
This is the only dissertation, or thesis, on Emily
Dickinson to come out of Austria and no book seems
to have been published on her. It is
Granichstaedten-Czerva's opinion that "Emily was
born in a poetic vacuum" (p. 116). She was

Also in 1945, Ada M. Klett published "Doom and Fortitude: A Study of Poetic Metaphor in Annette von Droste-Hülshoff (1797-1848) and Emily Dickinson (1830-1886)" in Monatshefte für Deutschen Unterricht.[15] The title clearly indicates that the essay is devoted to a comparison between the two poets. There is a detailed description of the upper middle-class background of both poetesses and also of other biographical similarities. Klett sees an unhappy love experience as the determining factor in the literary output of both: the two "determine that a deathblow to their love shall become a stimulant to their art."[16] Klett remarks that the women share "an acute awareness" and a "sensuous perception," but in Dickinson's case, this awareness takes the form of conscious introspection. Klett considers this introspection "a legacy of her [Dickinson's] Puritan heritage," something Droste did not share. According to Klett, the common denominator in the poetry of the two women is a sense of doom: in Droste, there is no help, Christian or otherwise, but in Dickinson, the doom generates fortitude. Klett suggests that the basic difference between

---

"totally uninfluenced" by any other poet; even "Puritanism hardly influenced her work" (p. 116), an opinion not shared by many critics. Granichstaedten-Czerva concentrates on synesthesia and the work of Dickinson: "the many colors of nature . . . [play] the greatest role as synesthesia in her poetry" (p. 102). Most pages are devoted to a predictable evaluation of Dickinson's use of colors; thus, purple connotes "something high and dignified (p. 106)," and so on.

[15]Ada M. Klett, "Doom and Fortitude: A Study of Poetic Metaphor in Annette von Droste-Hülshoff (1797-1848) and Emily Dickinson (1830-1886)," Monatshefte für Deutschen Unterricht, 37 (1945), 37-54.

[16]Klett, p. 38.

the poetesses is how they cope with being doomed. Dickinson is the stronger individual and in her poetry, somehow "the soul faces the foe." This quality gives her poetry a healing power and it is this very quality that makes Dickinson's poetry great, Klett concludes her article. Other than Droste-Hülshoff, Klett mentions only one other possible German parallel to Dickinson, Heine: the common denominator here is their humor.[17]

Josef Frank, contrary to Granichstaedten-Czerva but in agreement with Klett, saw Dickinson as a Puritan, who never could escape that heritage.[18] According to Frank, Dickinson's "love" first and last regards nature. The fact that she was so close to nature is related to the fact that she stayed a child all her life: she "was never to become a woman," in Frank's euphemistic words. He maintains that this trait is responsible for her intense interest in the small domestic things in life, a reaction one would expect from a child. Frank reserves his highest praise for the linguistic vitality of Dickinson's poetry. Her "magic art" is "bold"; she turned all of life into "allegories."[19] The caprices of her language, the emancipation from rules, and the fragmented, abrupt expression were her gifts to the Imagists, Frank concludes.

World War II was over and the German people slowly turned from the harsh realities of living and dying to the more pleasant ones of reading. The latest thing in the publishing world was the appearance of pocket books, up to this point almost unknown in Germany. The fifties saw a steady

[17]Cf. chapter II, footnotes 42 and 63, where Dickinson is also compared to Heine.

[18]Josef Frank, "Emily Dickinson," _Prisma_, 6 (April 1947), 21-23.

[19]Frank, p. 23.

increase in publications in all fields. The first
Emily Dickinson publication in the fifties was J.
Wesley Thomas' Amerikanische Dichter und Die
Deutsche Literatur [American Poets and German Lit-
erature].[20] Less than a page is devoted to Emily
Dickinson but Thomas called for "the most successful pioneer . . . of the nineteenth century."
Thomas observes that she is close to the American
poets of the present century, and naturally so,
since she was "an experimentalist in verse." The
general thesis of the book is to attempt to prove
that many American poets, among them Dickinson,
were familiar with German literature. One suggested influence on Dickinson is Heine: the general
realism, the disappointment in life, and the sudden changes of a sombre mood to a flippant one are
some of the parallels that suggest this influe-
ence.[21] Thomas cites no specific poems or lines
to back up his reasoning.

In 1952, Henry Lüdeke published Geschichte
der Amerikanischen Literatur [History of American
Literature].[22] Lüdeke sees the language of "one
of the great poetesses of world literature [Emily
Dickinson]" as typical of the "practical, laconi-
cal, and careful" mind behind New England popular
literature, particularly the literature of the
church: maximal meaning made to fit a minimal
package. Lüdeke observes that while this kind of
communication demands precision--the major attrac-

[20]J. Wesley Thomas, Amerikanische Dichter und
die Deutsche Literatur (Duderstadt: Volksbücherei
Verlag Goslar, 1950), pp. 110-11.

[21]Cf. comments on Heine, footnote 17.

[22]Henry Lüdeke, Geschichte der Amerikanischen
Literatur (Bern: A. Francke Verlag, 1952), pp.
352-56. Lüdeke is professor at Universität Basel,
Switzerland, one of the few German-speaking scholars of this chapter who is not from Germany
proper.

139

tion of Dickinson's poetry--it also allows for
freedom from rules in syntax, even vocabulary. It
is Lüdeke's opinion that Dickinson did not want to
publish because she knew that the form of her poetry was "consciously sacrificed to the message."
It is this form, Lüdeke continues, that would appeal to later generations of American poets.
Lüdeke adds that her humor, above all her habit of
co-ordinating the familiar with the dignified and
the worldly with the godly, places her in the
tradition of Mark Twain.[23] Lüdeke is one of the
few European critics who sees Dickinson as a specifically American phenomenon. Speaking of the
content of her poetry, Lüdeke remarks that Dickinson's "unfulfilled love experience" is the
strongest factor behind her literary production.
He also praises her religious poetry and considers
her belief extraordinarily strong: "truth is
beauty," as he puts it.[24]

In 1953, Julius Bab published a small collection of translated Dickinson poems, twelve in
all.[25]

[23]The same quality in Dickinson's poetry has
led others to compare her to Heine; see, for instance, footnotes 17 and 21.

[24]Cf. chapter II, footnotes 96 and 97, dealing with the Keatsian sense of "truth is beauty."

[25]Julius Bab, Amerikas neuere Lyrik [Modern
American Poetry] (Bad Nauheim: [no publ.], 1953),
pp. 49-53. The twelve poems are: "Ins offne Ohr
klar sprechen mir die Blätter" ["To my quick ear
the Leaves--conferred"]; "Ich zog einen Wechsel
aufs Leben" ["I took one Draught of Life"]; "Hörst
Du die Neuigkeiten?" ["The Only News I know"];
"Des Heimchens Schrei" ["The Crickets sang"]; "Ich
bin niemand--wer bist du?" ["I'm Nobody! Who are
you?"]; "Von allen Seelen, die Gott schuf" ["Of
all the Souls that stand create"]; "Kein Schiff
vermag uns wie ein Buch" ["There is no Frigate

In _Anglia_, Ruth Schirmer-Imhoff wrote a review-article concerning the Mabel Loomis Todd
edition of Dickinson's letters.[26] According to
Schirmer-Imhoff, the quality of Dickinson's letters more than matches that of her poetry: in
both, Dickinson shows the "exaggerated sensitivi-
ty" that was her "fate." Her ability to see
greater implications behind everyday things, such
as flowers and bees, is the same in both prose
and poetry. Schirmer-Imhoff, like many other critics, places Dickinson solidly in the tradition of
English seventeenth-century literature. The fact
that the Todd edition of letters offers a genuine
"whole picture of the writer [Dickinson]" is not
so much thanks to the editor as to the poetess,
Schirmer-Imhoff concludes her review.

Franz Link, in 1954, published an article on
Dickinson called "Vier Gedichte Emily Dickinsons"
["Four Poems by Emily Dickinson"].[27] The four
poems ("I like to see it lap the Miles"; "My Life
had stood--a Loaded Gun"; "Although I put away his
life"; and "After great pain, a formal feeling

---

like a Book"]; "Schon zweimal schloss vor seinem
Schluss" ["My life closed twice before its close"];
"Das Herz wünscht erst sich Lust" ["The Heart asks
Pleasure--first"]; "Die Fliege summte, als ich
starb" ["I heard a Fly buzz--when I died"]; "Wenn
die Rotkehlchen wiederkommen" ["If I should'nt be
alive"]; and "Sicher in alabasternen Räumen"
["Safe in their Alabaster Chambers"].

[26] Mabel Loomis Todd, ed., _Letters of Emily_
Dickinson, rev. by Ruth Schirmer-Imhoff, _Anglia_,
71 (1953), 365-66. The edition of letters
referred to is Mabel Loomis Todd, ed., _Letters of_
Emily Dickinson (Cleveland: World Publishing
Company, 1951).

[27] Franz Link, "Vier Gedichte Emily Dickinsons," _Die Neueren Sprachen_, 3 (1954), 406-13.

comes") are presented in English. The interpretations would fall under the heading of linguistic explications de texte. Of the German works surveyed in this study, this is the first to use a linguistic approach, although in Germany, this method of interpretation has traditionally been favored over others. Link carefully discusses versification, rhymes, and syntax; from this material he draws psychological conclusions. From the vantage point of today, the interpretations are predictable. For instance, "I like to see it lap the Miles" is seen as a tribute to a new railroad. Link makes the remark that only a close reading of Dickinson's "successful poems" can tell us the value of the poetry; "scholarly criticism has suffered . . . [at the hands of] her over-devoted admirers." After giving his reading of "My Life had stood--a Loaded Gun" (a death wish), "Although I put away his life" (a love poem closely resembling those of the Middle Ages), and "After great pain, a formal feeling comes" (a religious poem), Link concludes that despite the fact that Dickinson's world is limited, there are a depth and an immediacy of feeling that place her above most American poets.

In 1955, Hans Hennecke published six translations of Dickinson poems in a full-length poetry collection: three were reprints from his 1937 publication and three were additions. The book is called Gedichte von Shakespeare bis Ezra Pound [Poetry from Shakespeare to Ezra Pound].[28] The critical comments are identical to those of 1937.

Hans Combecher's Muse in Amerika: Vom eigen-

[28]Hans Hennecke, Gedichte von Shakespeare bis Ezra Pound (Wiesbaden: Limes, 1955), pp. 254-61. The three added poems are: "Der Tod--das ist ein lang' Gespräch" ["Death is a Dialogue between"]; "Ärzte müssen sich inmitten" ["Surgeons must be very careful"]; and "Schau auf die Zeit versöhnten Augs" ["Look back on Time, with kindly eyes"].

willigen Weg amerikanischer Dichtung. Interpretationen [The Muse in America: The Independent Road
of American Poetry: Interpretations] appeared as
a booklet, or a supplement, published by Die
Neueren Sprachen.[29] Combecher gives sophisticated
explications de texte of four poems; he remarks
that the best tribute to Dickinson's art is the
fact that where she needs so few words, her interpreters need many.[30] It is Combecher's thesis
that Dickinson is a true believer in God. He comments on the "recipe formula" of "To make a prairie it takes a clover and one bee": "Whoever publishes a recipe must have tried it out himself."
Combecher sees no bitterness or self-indulgence
in "I never lost as much but twice"; on the contrary, God has helped twice and he will do it
again. Finally, "I never saw a Moor" is seen as
the epitome of solid belief. Our concepts of the
next world, Combecher argues, are based on what
our experience in this world has taught us; inas-
much as this experience lets us understand even
what we have not seen--such as a moor--we are likewise allowed to conceive of what is beyond this
life. And this is Dickinson's greatness, Combecher
suggests: from knowledge of everyday facts comes
the vision of a world yet unseen. "This wonder of
transformation Emily Dickinson manages [to create]
in almost all her poems" in Combecher's evaluation.

An important book, for its size if nothing
else, is Maria Mathi's Der Engel in Grau: Aus dem
Leben und Werk der amerikanischen Dichterin Emily
Dickinson [The Angel in Gray: From the Life and

[29]Hans Combecher, Muse in Amerika: Vom eigen-
willigen Weg amerikanischer Dichtung. Interpretationen. Die Neueren Sprachen, Supplement I
(n.d.), pp. 13-23.

[30]The four poems are: "To make a prairie it
takes a clover and one bee"; "These are the days
when Birds come back"; "I never lost as much but
twice"; and "I never saw a Moor."

Work of the American Poetess Emily Dickinson].[31]
The book contains letters as well as poetry with a
brief critical commentary on both. Mathi argues
that Dickinson's poems are "hidden in gray": the
content of the poems is like "a flame" and once
noticed, it outweighs "the gray" of her "imperfect
rhymes." Mathi goes on to say that it is "regret-
table" that Dickinson did not attempt to better
"the technique of her art." Nevertheless, before
Dickinson's lifetime, the United States had certainly not produced any poetry comparable to hers.
Mathi observes that two things meant everything to
Dickinson: nature and religion. Everything in
life, including death, is observed by the poet in
a detached, philosophical way, Mathi concludes.
Mathi's comments on the letters concern mainly the
persons involved in the correspondence; that Mathi
admires Dickinson's letters is implied. There are
fifty poems, all in Mathi's translation.

     In 1959, another woman, Lola Gruenthal, pub-
lished her translations of thirty-six Dickinson
poems, Emily Dickinson: Gedichte [Emily Dickinson: Poems].[32] The fact that two such substantial
collections came out within three years testifies
to the solid appreciation of Dickinson's poetry in
the fifties on the part of German critics, and
also of the nation itself. In her critical comments, Gruenthal observes that while we still know
nothing about Dickinson's "unknown beloved," we do
know what is important: the quality of her poetry.
Thanks to Mrs. Todd, Dickinson can be considered
"the most important poetess of the English language." Gruenthal continues: "The passion for
realization . . . is what invests her poetry with
a genuine beauty." Gruenthal remarks that compared

     [31]Der Engel in Grau: Aus dem Leben und Werk
der amerikanischen Dichterin Emily Dickinson, ed.
and trans. Maria Mathi (Mannheim: Kessler, 1956).

     [32]Emily Dickinson: Gedichte, ed. and trans.
Lola Gruenthal (Berlin: Henssel, 1959).

to Dickinson's poetry, other poetic products,
perhaps more "perfect," seem like "hot-house
plants." Gruenthal pays tribute to the Harvard
edition of 1955 which she has closely followed in
her own translations. She concludes her brief remarks by stating that, to a German reader, Dickinson seems "an American reincarnation of Heine," an
opinion shared by many German critics.

Also in 1959, Leo Spitzer, in an article devoted to Charles Baudelaire, "Baudelaire's
'Spleen,'" saw an occasion to include some observations on Emily Dickinson.[33] Professor Spitzer
remarks that "the basic mood of the poem ["Spleen"]
is in accordance with Baudelaire's work as a whole
in that the feeling of claustration [sic] in a
tomb . . . is a motif that constantly recurs with
him." Spitzer goes on to observe that, apparently,
"salvation can be achieved only by the transfig-
uration of his 'misery' into artistic beauty."
Dickinson's poem "I felt a Funeral, in my Brain"
offers "striking similarities with Baudelaire's
'Spleen,'" Spitzer suggests. Her feeling, however,
is more related to the intellect than to emotion.
Despite the similarities suggested, Spitzer sees
some distinct differences in the way the two poets
handle the material: Dickinson, as always, is
understated, using none of the pompe funèbre that
Baudelaire loved. Spitzer concludes that Dickinson is "indebted to Puritan intellectual and personal mysticism" and Baudelaire, of course, is
very far from that.[34]

In the same year, Inge Meidinger-Geise wrote

---

[33]Leo Spitzer, "Baudelaire's 'Spleen,'"
Romanische Literaturstudien (Tübingen: Max
Niemeyer Verlag, 1959), pp. 286-93. Subsequent
references to this article will be cited as
"Spleen."

[34]Spitzer, "Spleen," p. 202.

a short review-article for <u>Welt und Wort</u>.[35]
Meidinger-Geise briefly reviews Gruenthal's translations. She considers them more of an inducement
to reading Dickinson than genuinely first-rate
translations. Meidinger-Geise observes that "this
outstanding North-American poetess" is difficult
to translate: there are too many seeming contra-
dictions in her poetry for a translator's task to
be an easy one. There are, for instance, the "re-
signed voice," the "naive begging voice," and "the
angrily revealing voice." The dichotomy of the I
and the world is the common denominator in all of
Dickinson's poetry, Meidinger-Geise concludes her
article.

Again in the same year, Werner Vordtriede
published "Die Puritanische Droste" ["The Puritan
Droste"], another comparison between Dickinson and
Annette von Droste-Hülshoff.[36] In part, this
article is also a review of Gruenthal's Dickinson
translations. The article is heavily biased in
favor of Catholicism: "she [Droste] looked further,
into another world, close to this world, as Catho-
lics do, instead of constantly listening to what
is within, in Protestant misery."[37] Nevertheless,
Vordtriede has the highest regard for Dickinson,
a regard more for the content than the form of her
poetry. According to him she was filled with rebellion; in addition, her mind is ironic and keen.
Vordtriede is critical of the form of her poetry;
she is called "consciously provincial, vague in
grammatical matters." It is his opinion that precisely on account of this lack of formal precision,

[35]Lola Gruenthal, <u>Emily Dickinson: Gedichte</u>,
rev. by Inge Meidinger-Geise, <u>Welt und Wort</u>, 14
(1959), 349.

[36]Werner Vordtriede, "Die Puritanische Droste,"
<u>Neue Deutsche Hefte</u>, 6 (December 1959), 857-59.

[37]Vordtriede, p. 857.

Dickinson's poetry lends itself ideally to translation.[38] He gives--contrary to Meidinger-Geise--high marks to Gruenthal as a translator.
Vordtriede concludes his article by giving a detailed linguistic critique of some finer points in Gruenthal's translations.[39]

Perhaps the most significant decade in German Emily Dickinson criticism is the sixties. In January of 1960, Kurt Oppens published "Emily Dickinson: Überlieferung und Prophetie" ["Emily Dickinson: Tradition and Prophecy"].[40] Oppens concentrates on what he considers major aspects of Dickinson's poetry: Puritan religion balanced by religious skepticism. "Her work represents quite a tragic journey which starts in the Christian tradition and, via Kierkegaard and Rilke, ends in the deserts of Nietzsche."[41] Dickinson seems to be the Kierkegaard of poetry. Oppens continues that it is true that she was not conscious of sin, as Kierkegaard was, but all the other ingredients typical of Kierkegaard's world are there: the paradox of belief and disbelief, the dualism of man and God, plus the refusal to find compromises or easy solutions. Oppens sees Dickinson as the true manifestation of the new continent: she despises authority and sees her own self as detached from her surroundings rather than part of a tradition. Oppens observes that one is reminded of the "traditional role of the 'dissenter' in the Anglo-Saxon cultures" and he cites Poe, Melville, Hawthorne, and Thoreau as examples. Oppens is par-

[38]Most critics, and indeed translators, disagree.

[39]It is obviously Vordtriede's opinion that Gruenthal has missed some connotations of English words.

[40]Kurt Oppens, "Emily Dickinson: Überlieferung und Prophetie," Merkur, 14 (January 1960), 17-40.

[41]Oppens, p. 18.

ticularly impressed with Dickinson's language.
Her freedom in using grammar, syntax, and rhyme is
all admirable. Particularly impressive Oppens
considers Dickinson's use of the two great sources
of the English language, Anglo-Saxon and Latin.
In this use, Oppens sees her as vastly superior to
Rilke who was more successful when using Germanic
vocabulary. Oppens adds that the beauty of Dickinson's language is basically only a means to an
end—to articulate her religious experience,
whether in Puritan belief or ironic disbelief.
Oppens observes that whereas Droste-Hülshoff considers doubt an illness in itself, to Dickinson
doubt was the very essence of truth. Rather than
continuing the comparison of Dickinson to Droste-
Hülshoff, however, Oppens prefers to trace the
parallel between Dickinson and Rilke. There is
the obvious similarity of imagery but, above all,
there 'is the similar relationship to life in general. In what Oppens considers Dickinson's "an-
guished poems," he sees her as close to Nietzsche.
Nietzsche considered himself "crucified" and she
saw herself as the "Queen of Calvary." Oppens
concludes that the value of Dickinson's poetry,
particularly with regard to modern American poetry,
can hardly be exaggerated.

In 1961, Charlotte Iklé published an article,
"Sag Alles Wahr, Doch Sag Es Schräg" ["Tell all the
Truth but tell it slant"].[42] In the biographical
comments, Iklé observes that it is hardly important who Dickinson's unknown beloved was; what .
matters is the isolation that followed. This isolation might indicate a spiritual poverty to some;
in reality, Iklé argues, it represents "a widening
of dimensions" for somebody whose poetry made "the
scheme of time burst." Iklé maintains that to
Dickinson, individual experience is representative

[42]Charlotte Iklé, "Sag Alles Wahr, Doch Sag
Es Schräg," Du, Schweizerische Monatsschrift
[Zürich], 21 (1961), 63-64. Iklé is Swiss.

of universal experience. Precision is her instrument and here she differs from a Hopkins or a Dylan Thomas in their "bombastic rhetoric." The pervasive mood of Dickinson's poetry is doubt and it is probably this quality that makes her poetry timeless. Iklé concludes: "Emily Dickinson meant to poetry what Debussy did to music, and Monet to painting; the breaking-up of predictable patterns to form new ones in half-tones."

In "The Shape of American Poetry" published in Jahrbuch für Amerikastudien, Earl Rovit considered the works of "representative" poets: Edgar Allan Poe, Walt Whitman, Emily Dickinson, Robert Frost, T. S. Eliot, and Wallace Stevens.[43] To explain his selection, he uses three criteria: each poet has "created a substantial oeuvre," each has his own "voice," and each has "achieved some kind of popularity." Rovit has set out to discredit any "two-tradition theory" (poets as "introverted" -"extroverted"; poets who "commit their poetry in crepe-hung studies with the delight of subversive alchemists, while others flaunt their indiscretions publically"). Instead, Rovit suggests new prototypes. One he calls "the poet-as-ironist" (Poe, but, above all, Frost) and another category is "the poet-as-image-maker." In the second category, Rovit's examples are Dickinson and Stevens. The poet-as-image-maker, according to Rovit, is one who creates poems of objectivity, creates images that exist "beyond the authority of the poet's personal experience." Dickinson, Rovit suggests, attains "a near superhuman lucidity of vision." His example is "There's a certain Slant of light." In this kind of poem, the poet as such, as creator, hardly exists. The vision attained, Rovit concludes, has a life all its own.

In 1961, Leo Spitzer published "Baudelaire,

[43]Earl Rovit, "The Shape of American Poetry," Jahrbuch für Amerikastudien, 6 (Heidelberg: Carl Winter Universitätsverlag, 1961), 122-33.

Les Fleurs du Mal: LXXVII--Spleen."[44] The chapter is not a precise reprint but almost identical to Spitzer's publication of 1959 and, therefore, need not be commented on here.

Teut Andreas Riese's essay "Das Gestaltungsprinzip der Konkretion in der neueren amerikanischen Lyrik" ["The Creative Principle of Concreteness in the New American Poetry"] appeared in 1963.[45] Riese initially states that one of the main tasks of literary scholarship is to be able to regard a work as both autonomous and as part of a certain development. According to Riese, some poets can only be seen in one of these aspects. Longfellow, for instance, may certainly be seen as part of a tradition, but he offers nothing that is original. On the other hand, there are poets such as Poe, Whitman, and Dickinson. Riese observes that between these three, there are few connections, other than being "radical." One thing that the pathfinder-poets do have in common, Riese argues, is the principle of concreteness and, again, he mentions three particular names: Thoreau, Dickinson, and Frost. Thoreau's language, Riese continues, "is characterized by economy and clari-

[44]Leo Spitzer, "Baudelaire, Les Fleurs du Mal: LXXVII--Spleen," Interpretationen zur Geschichte der französischen Lyrik [Interpretations of the History of French Poetry] (Heidelberg: Selbstverlag des Romanischen Seminars der Universität Heidelberg, 1961), pp. 170-79.

[45]Teut Andreas Riese, "Das Gestaltungsprinzip der Konkretion in der neueren amerikanischen Lyrik," Jahrbuch für Amerikastudien, 8 (Heidelberg: Carl Winter Universitätsverlag, 1963), 136-47. Among Professor Riese's publications are: "The Idea of Evil in American and European Literature"; "Geschichtsverständnis und Geschichtsdichtung in Amerika des 20. Jahrhunderts" ["Sense of History and Poetry of History in Twentieth-Century America"]; and "The Golden Bow?".

ty" (the example is "Pray to what earth does this sweet cold belong") but the same is true for Frost ("The Road Not Taken"). But of the poets mentioned, Riese has more praise for Dickinson than for the others. The poem by her which he has chosen to explicate is "Glass was the Street--in tinsel Peril." Riese argues that "the present" of this winter scene is only there to accentuate "the past": "The Past's supreme italic." In other words, Dickinson's interest lies with the moment that is almost, but not quite, past, as if the essence of life were hidden at that crucial point. Riese suggests that this is Dickinson's "principle of concreteness": the tangible and the present are here, stressed in the poem only to point up the intangible that is just about to disappear. This back-and-forth movement between "solid" and "evaporating" is typical of Dickinson, Riese observes. This is her "concreteness" and it is as a master of catching the uncatchable that she has appealed to poets of a later century. Riese concludes his article by suggesting that, to an American, the land itself and all other "reality" are products of his own thinking and will-power. This, then, is the dividing line between the typical autonomous American poet and his European counterpart who sees himself as a product of his land and its heritage.[46] Emily Dickinson is one of the prime examples of this "new" American poet, a poet of concreteness.

Still in the same year, Riese wrote another article, "Emily Dickinson und der Sprachgeist amerikanischer Lyrik" ["Emily Dickinson and the Voice of American Poetry"].[47] Here, Riese concentrates on Dickinson's particular brand of religi-

[46]Similar thoughts had already been expressed by Oppens; see footnote 41.

[47]Teut Andreas Riese, "Emily Dickinson und der Sprachgeist amerikanischer Lyrik," Die Neueren Sprachen, 12 (1963), 145-59.

osity. Riese observes that biographical information helps not at all in getting to know an artist;
it is within "the realm of the religious experience" that we get to know Emily Dickinson. In an
explication de texte of "Those--dying then," Riese
suggests that it is the distance from God that
haunts Dickinson, not the non-existence. She had
lost the traditional belief in original sin and
other Puritan concepts. What she did have was the
ability to judge independently and stick to her
choice. Riese argues that the dynamics of Dickinson's poetry stems from this constant independent
searching for God, more precisely from the very
"insecurity of the searcher." Closely related to
this thesis, Riese continues, are the mainly linguistic explications of some Dickinson poems, such
as "Tell all the Truth but tell it slant": the
real truth is so blinding that it kills. As human
beings, we have to find a "slant" way of approach-
ing God. So much of Dickinson's poetry leads, directly and logically, to a language not only
"slant" but so economic in expression that it almost ceases to flow: language itself may no longer
be sufficient. Thus, the epigrammatic quality of
Dickinson's poetry is logical although it may
strike the reader as "radical," a radicalism which
is part of the new "American poetic voice," Riese
concludes his article.

1968 saw several publications on Emily Dickinson. Martin Schulze wrote Wege der amerikanischen Literatur: Eine geschichtliche Darstellung
[The Paths of American Literature: A Historical
Approach].[48] Schulze calls Dickinson "one of the
most unconventional and important poetesses of
America." All of the things that we now consider
typical of twentieth-century poetry are to be
found in her poetry: "the bold symbolism, the
ethereal impressionism, [and] the hard realism,"

[48]Martin Schulze, Wege der amerikanischen
Literatur: Eine geschichtliche Darstellung
(Frankfurt am Main: Ullstein, 1968), pp. 185-88.

152

Schulze comments. He adds that in Dickinson's poetry, the language itself is synonymous with the
experience. According to Schulze, Dickinson never
escaped Puritanism, even though she is definitely
closer to the Metaphysical poets of the seventeenth century. She is a realist and as such
often witty and ironic. Traces of her poetry can
be found everywhere in the works of Pound, Amy
Lowell, and Richard Aldington. Not the breadth of
an all-human experience but the depth of metaphysical problem-solving within one individual constitutes the greatness of her work, Schulze sums up.

Klaus Lubbers' important work Der literarische
Ruhm Emily Dickinsons: Das erste Jahrhundert
amerikanischer und britischer Kritik von Werk und
Mensch [The Literary Reputation of Emily Dickinson: The First Century of American and British
Criticism of the Work and the Individual] was published in Germany in 1967. In 1968, he published
the work in English under the title of Emily Dickinson: The Critical Revolution.[49] Since the book
is available in English, it will only be briefly

[49]Klaus Lubbers, Emily Dickinson: The Criti-
cal Revolution (Ann Arbor: University of Michigan
Press, 1968). Klaus Lubbers is professor at
Universität Mainz. Among his publications are:
Die Todesszene und ihre Funktion im Kurzgeschich-
tenwerk von Edgar Allan Poe [The Death Scene and
Its Function in the Short Stories of Edgar Allan
Poe]; Zwei Klassiker der amerikanischen Kurz-
geschichte: Interpretationen zu Edgar Allan Poe
und Ernest Hemingway [Two Classics of the American
Short Story: Interpretations of Edgar Allan Poe
and Ernest Hemingway; in collaboration with
Galinsky]; "Irving: 'Rip van Winkle'"; "Zur Rezep-
tion der amerikanischen Kurzgeschichte in Deutsch-
land nach 1945" ["The Reception of the American
Short Story in Germany after 1945"]; "Tennessee
Williams"; "John Updikes [sic] 'Rabbit Run'"; and
"The Necessary Order: A Study of Theme and Structure in Carson McCullers' Fiction."

153

commented on here, despite the fact that it represents, to date, the fullest effort devoted solely
to Emily Dickinson on the part of any European
scholar.[50] Not only does Professor Lubbers trace
all of the scholarly criticism from 1862 to 1962
originating either in the United States or England,
but the study also deals with such divergent aspects as the role played by major American Dickinson scholars within the body of criticism, her appearance (and the implications thereof) in anthol-
ogies at different times, dramas written about her
life, poems set to music, and a wealth of other
material.

In the same year that the American version of
Klaus Lubbers' book appeared, Hans Galinsky published Wegbereiter Moderner Amerikanischer Lyrik:
Interpretations- und Rezeptionsstudien zu Emily
Dickinson und William Carlos Williams [Pathfinders
in Modern American Poetry: Studies in the Interpretation and Reception of Emily Dickinson and
William Carlos Williams].[51] Somewhat less than
half of the book is devoted to Dickinson. The sub-
chapter called "Emily Dickinson in Deutschland"
["Emily Dickinson in Germany"], together with the
Appendix, contains bibliographical and other information on publications in Germany, especially
in the field of translation.[52] Generally speaking,
Galinsky has attempted both an "intrinsic" study
of "the work as it is" and an "extrinsic" one as

[50]Brita Lindberg-Seyersted's full-length study
(see chapter II, footnote 119) is equally comprehensive. It is linguistically oriented whereas
Lubbers takes a historical approach.

[51]Galinsky, Wegbereiter (see footnote 2).

[52]A brief study of the relative merits of the
German translations was done by Sabine Reitmayer
in 1966. Galinsky's own comments on the various
items, when he offers any, are extremely brief.
His purpose is primarily historical.

154

the work was received. Professor Galinsky places
the emphasis on close, linguistically oriented
reading of a few poems chosen to represent nature,
God, and love. Galinsky's first example of classified poems is "I like to see it lap the Miles"
which he, like most critics, interprets as homage
to a new railroad.[53] His examples of "nature poems" are "The Sky is low--the Clouds are mean" and
"A Route of Evanescence." Among his examples of
religious poems are: "Lightly stepped a yellow
star" and "I never saw a Moor"; Galinsky, too,
sees a deep religious belief as the core of the
last poem.[54] In his learned explications of Dickinson's religious poems, Galinsky suggests many
sources other than the Bible, such as John Bunyan
and Richard Baxter. Galinsky observes that Baxter
is mentioned in one of Dickinson's letters but he
does not identify the letter. Of the "love poems,"
Galinsky mentions "Mine--by the Right of the White
Election!" and "A Charm invests a face." It is
Galinsky's opinion that religious and erotic experiences "blend" in Dickinson's poetry to a point
where they are truly one, an opinion shared by
several critics. The same, Galinsky argues, also
holds true for the religious poems and the ones
concerning nature, which he also finds pantheistic.
Galinsky sees Dickinson as representing the highest
point of development from Anne Bradstreet to Robert
Lowell: a poet of "the life of the mind." He also
places her in another context, namely as a representative of the kind of artistry in which "the
loneliness of [life's] circumstances parallels the

[53]It is interesting that Galinsky, in agreement with Robert Goffin (chapter IV), suggests
additional aspects of "I like to see it lap the
Miles." Thus, in discussing the animal imagery
of the poem, Galinsky observes: "To fit it's sides
can suggest two things: the pelvic area of a woman
and the flanks of a horse" (p. 62).

[54]Cf. Combecher's discussion of "I never saw
a Moor," footnote 30.

loneliness of imagination."[55]   Among several such
artists, Galinsky mentions Melville, Whitman, and
O'Neill, all of whom he finds closely related to
"the greatest poetess of the United States [Dick-
inson]."

The seventies started with a combined Liepe-
Lubbers publication: Emily Dickinson: Gedichte
[Emily Dickinson: Poems].[56] The book is a substantial selection of Dickinson's poems, one hundred
and twenty-nine. The fact that the book is a
paperback testifies to the standing of Emily Dickinson in Germany at the beginning of the latest
decade. In Lubbers' commentary, one first finds
general biographical information. Lubbers then
discusses what he terms "poems of definition." He
explains: "She was concerned with knowledge, truth
. . . [and] the establishment of order out of the
chaos of experience."[57] Lubbers calls Dickinson's
relationship with nature "problematical"; his example is "A little Madness in the Spring," where
the clown, not the king, has more understanding of
nature.[58] In Lubbers' words, "here man, there
nature" is the tragic formula for Dickinson's view
of nature. Regarding the religious poetry, Lubbers
observes that "she was never against the bible but
against its official interpreters." He adds that
Dickinson's relationship to God is as problematical

[55]Galinsky, Wegbereiter, p. 105. Cf. Emil
Staiger and "the theory of loneliness," chapter II,
footnote 100.

[56]Emily Dickinson: Gedichte, trans. Gertrud
Liepe, afterword, Klaus Lubbers (Stuttgart:
Phillips Reclam Jun., 1970).

[57]Cf. the passion for order often noticed in
Wallace Stevens.

[58]This poem is also a central one in the judgment of Lars von Haartman; see his translation,
frontispiece of this study.

as that to nature: it seems safe to assume that
the relationship became "increasingly skeptical"
in quality. Lubbers also discusses "Wild Nights--
Wild Nights!" and "Title divine--is mine!"; according to him, there is nothing to indicate whether
the poems regard "a lover, the muse, or God."[59]
Lubbers makes a passing reference to the similarities of humor found in Dickinson's poetry and in
Huckleberry Finn without elaborating the point.[60]
He concludes that Dickinson is "a genius, modern
and timeless at the same time, a victim of her
narrow life circumstances, [and] a rebel against
the Puritan tradition." ·

In ESQ, Roland Hagenbüchle published "Precision and Indeterminacy in the Poetry of Emily Dickinson."[61] Despite the fact that this article is
written in English, it nevertheless reflects a
German viewpoint of Dickinson's poetry by a major
European scholar and is therefore included here.
In a decidedly linguistically oriented discussion,
Professor Hagenbüchle concentrates on Dickinson's
"indeterminacy," which, according to him, may be
deliberate, even "decisive." Hagenbüchle remarks
that instead of concentrating on the objective
world, Dickinson concentrates on her own consciousness of it. In other words, although an effect is
recorded, the cause of it "remains an enigma."
Hagenbüchle suggests that overall, Dickinson "shows
a predilection for fading contours"; this is her

[59]Cf. Robert Goffin's viewpoint, chapter IV,
footnote 94.

[60]Cf. Lüdeke's comments on her sense of humor,
footnote 23.

[61]Roland Hagenbüchle, "Precision and Indeterminacy in the Poetry of Emily Dickinson," ESQ, 20
(1974), 33-56. Professor Hagenbüchle has recently
moved from Zürich, Switzerland, to Universität
Wuppertal, Germany.

deliberate choice.[62] Closely related to the above
is Hagenbüchle's discussion of what the French
Symbolists called absence présente, i.e., "ideal
presence in the mind presupposes absence in actu-
ality." Again, along the same lines as Riese,
Hagenbüchle argues that the most intense moment of
realization occurs only after an experience is
past. This is also how Hagenbüchle explains Dickinson's interest in death: only from a point very
near death does life reveal its significance. In
this respect, Hagenbüchle is not unlike other critics, in particular the French, who see Dickinson
as close to Mallarmé, Baudelaire, and Rilke. Thus,
the poetry of "one of the greatest poets of the
last century [Dickinson] is characterized by an
element of deliberate indeterminacy," Hagenbüchle
concludes.

The last German item to be treated in this
study is Die Amerikanische Lyrik: Von der Kolonialzeit bis zur Gegenwart [American Poetry: From Colonial Times to the Present] edited by Klaus
Lubbers.[63] This is a collection of essays, two of
which concern Dickinson, with a historically oriented introduction by Lubbers. Lubbers remarks
that nowadays not only names such as Emerson,
Longfellow, and Whitman are current in the world
of German literary criticism of American poetry
but also Poe, Frost, Pound, Dickinson, and Cummings. As a "pathfinder," Dickinson equals Whitman, Lubbers concludes his remarks.

Teut Andreas Riese is the author of both
articles on Emily Dickinson. In "Like Some Old
fashioned Miracle," where Riese attempts an ex-

[62]Cf. Riese's discussion of "Glass was the
Street--in tinsel Peril," footnote 46.

[63]Klaus Lubbers, "Einleitung," Die Ameri-
kanische Lyrik: Von der Kolonialzeit bis zur
Gegenwart, ed. Klaus Lubbers (Düsseldorf: August
Bagel Verlag, 1974), pp. 11-20.

plication of the poem of the same title, Riese
first discusses the difficulties that encounter
the Dickinson scholar because "there is no author-
ized text."[64] Even in the case of Johnson's 1955
edition, Riese argues that, for each single poem,
the scholar has to decide whether the version of
the poem found in the Johnson edition is the best
to follow or not. Riese then proceeds to the
thesis of his article, namely the absence présente
that he himself, Oppens, and Hagenbüchle had been
concerned with in previous articles: he stresses
the fact that the core of the title poem is the
"summer's recollection." One major aspect of the
past is that one cannot lose it; this is about as
near as the human being comes to "reality." In
discussing the structure of the poem, Riese sees a
parallel between the implications of the bitter-
sweetness of the dying summer and Dickinson's use
of children's stories within the poem. There are
Cinderella, Little John, and Blue Beard.
Cinderella and Little John have positive connotations: the reader is happy. Blue Beard strikes
another note. The reader is now faced with something "terrible" and "secretive," but, more than
that, with a hint of loss and of the "truth of
dying," all of which parallels the various psychological shades of summer. In addition, the tone
of the poem is "casual," even "nonchalant," Riese
remarks, and this is in line with Dickinson's
credo to tell the truth, but tell it slant.

The other article by Riese in the same publication is called "As imperceptibly as Grief."[65]

[64]Teut Andreas Riese, "Emily Dickinson: Like
Some Old fashioned Miracle," Die Amerikanische
Lyrik: Von der Kolonialzeit bis zur Gegenwart, ed.
Klaus Lubbers (Düsseldorf: August Bagel Verlag,
1974), pp. 147-56.

[65]Teut Andreas Riese, "Emily Dickinson: As
imperceptibly as Grief," Die Amerikanische Lyrik:
Von der Kolonialzeit bis zur Gegenwart, ed. Klaus

In a sense, this article is a companion piece to
the above-mentioned article; it, too, concentrates
on the absence présente. As far as the actual
title poem is concerned, the linguistic interpretation is in many ways a rewritten version of the
remarks on that poem in the before-mentioned
"Emily Dickinson und der Sprachgeist amerikanischer
Lyrik" and, therefore, need not be commented on
here.

There remain to be considered two representative reference works. In 1968, Brockhaus Enzyklopädie carried a highly appreciative entry on Emily
Dickinson.[66] Following some brief biographical
information, the anonymous writer goes on to de-
scribe Dickinson's poetry about "love and death"
as "alive and paradoxical, of a beauty that tears
[the reader] apart." Dickinson is placed in the
tradition of the Metaphysical poets, in particular
Donne and Vaughn [sic], and called "the greatest
poetess of America." Among critical works mentioned are those of Whicher, Chase, and Leyda.

In Meyers Enzyklopädisches Lexikon, nature
and "Puritan self-analysis" are called Dickinson's
major preoccupations.[67] Her belief in God is tem-
pered by an inclination toward skepticism, even
anguish. Her poems are "tart" and "economic in
expression"; today, she is considered "the most
important American poetess." Anderson and Leyda
are among the few Dickinson critics mentioned.

Lubbers (Düsseldorf: August Bagel Verlag, 1974),
pp. 157-62.

[66]Brockhaus Enzyklopädie (Wiesbaden: F. A.
Brockhaus, 1968), IV, 708.

[67]Meyers Enzyklopädisches Lexikon (Mannheim:
Bibliographisches Institut, 1972), VI, 761.

Summary of German Criticism of Emily Dickinson

The first criticism of Emily Dickinson in the German language was written by a German-American and published in a German newspaper in Chicago in 1898 (see footnotes 3-5). The article offers what is possibly the first translations of Dickinson poetry into a foreign tongue. It also anticipates German Dickinson criticism by referring to the poet as "a genius" and comparing her to the German poetess Annette von Droste-Hülshoff.

Some few but significant critical items from Germany on Dickinson appeared between 1898 and the mid-forties. In 1928, Keller and Fehr see the poet as a perfect example of transcendentalism, a viewpoint shared by few critics, but they also call her influence on modern American poetry "immense" (see footnote 7). In the same year, a poem of Dickinson is used to preface an article in a German magazine for psychology. Apparently, the author considers Dickinson too well known to need an introduction in the context (see footnote 8). Two years later, Friedrich Bruns gives his opinion that Dickinson and Crane are contemporary poets and thus belong in his book on American contemporary poetry (see footnote 9). Bruns has reservations about Dickinson's style but is otherwise anticipating later criticism: he calls her "a visionary." In Hans Hennecke's pre-World War II article, Dickinson's language is particularly praised for the first time (see footnote 11). She is called "perhaps the finest poetess since Sappho."

The forties, especially the years prior to the end of World War II, offered very little Dickinson criticism. Schirmer, in a literary history published in 1945, considers Dickinson's style "undeveloped"; however, he still sees her in the tradition of the Metaphysical poets and as the great forerunner of twentieth-century American poetry (see footnote 13). In the same year, Ada M. Klett extensively compares Dickinson and Droste-Hülshoff; the tertium comparationis is their

sense of doom and how they handle it (see footnote
15). Dickinson is called the superior one of the
two poets. Klett is also the first of the critics
in this survey to compare Dickinson to Heine, a
suggestion that was to recur again and again in
later German criticism. Josef Frank emphasizes
Dickinson's stylistic virtuosity (see footnote 18).
Her "fragmented" art is now called "magic" and her
poetry is viewed as a major legacy to the Imagists.

The fifties saw a marked increase in Dickinson
criticism. Out of twelve items surveyed, there
were two full-length books devoted to Dickinson
(see footnotes 31 and 32). The other items were
either articles, parts of books, or, in three cases,
review-articles. J. Wesley Thomas, in his book of
1950, devotes little space to Dickinson (see footnote 20). He is, however, highly complimentary.
Dickinson is called "the most successful pioneer
. . . of the nineteenth century," second not even
to Whitman. It is Dickinson's experimentation with
form that particularly impresses Thomas. Henry
Lüdeke, two years later, also sees the form of
Dickinson's poetry as the most outstanding aspect
(see footnote 22). He regards her as a specifically American blend of qualities: the practical and
the careful, mixed with a sense of humor à la Mark
Twain. Contrary to this viewpoint, Ruth Schirmer-
Imhoff, in a review-article of the Todd edition of
Dickinson's letters, sees the poet as a late product of a British seventeenth-century tradition
(see footnote 26). In 1954, Franz Link is the
first of the Germans in this survey to use a linguistic approach to interpretation, a method traditionally favored by Germans (see footnote 27).
Link sees Dickinson as more "natural" and "immediate" than other American poets. Hans Combecher,
in the mid-fifties, sets out to prove his thesis
that Dickinson's belief in God was the overall
determining factor in her writing of poetry (see
footnote 29). Maria Mathi's book on Dickinson of
1956 was the first full-length study devoted to
the poet (see footnote 31). It is also the first
substantial collection of translated Dickinson

poems. Mathi reserves her appreciation mainly for the "message" of the poetry rather than for the form. The next important Dickinson item of the decade is a full-length book, also written by a woman, and also a collection of translated poetry (see footnote 32). Lola Gruenthal places emphasis on "the passion for realization" (an idea close to Klaus Lubbers' reading of what he terms "poems of definition"; see footnote 56) which, according to her, invests Dickinson's poetry with genuine life. Gruenthal also stresses the parallel to Heinrich Heine with regard to his particular brand of humor. Leo Spitzer's article sees a parallel between Baudelaire and Dickinson (see footnote 33). Their realm of interest is much the same, both frequently using funerals and tombs as subject matter. However, their linguistic approaches differ: Baudelaire evokes pompe funèbre whereas Dickinson is intellectual and low-keyed in her approach. Werner Vordtriede marks the end of the decade by a return to the comparison between Dickinson and Droste-Hülshoff (see footnote 36). Vordtriede is critical of the form of Dickinson's poetry but enthusiastic with regard to her ironic and keen mind.

The sixties saw the best known German Anglicisten contributing to Dickinson criticism. Names such as Klaus Lubbers, Hans Galinsky, Kurt Oppens, and Teut Andreas Riese are to be found, to be followed later (1974) by Roland Hagenbüchle. Of the nine items of the sixties considered here, one was a full-length book (see footnote 49), one half of a full-length book (see footnote 51), one part of a book, and the other ones articles. Kurt Oppens, opening the decade, concentrates on the question of belief versus disbelief in Dickinson: he sees parallels in particular to Søren Kierkegaard, but also to Rilke and Nietzsche (see footnote 40). Oppens is particularly impressed with all aspects of Dickinson's language, from syntax to vocabulary. Charlotte Iklé compares the "half-tones" of Dickinson's language to those of Debussy and Monet, masters of the "language" in their respective

163

fields (see footnote 42). Earl Rovit, still in
the early sixties, labels Dickinson and Wallace
Stevens the "poet-as-image-maker," i.e., a poet
who creates, objectively, images that exist "beyond the authority of the poet's personal experience" (see footnote 43). Teut Andreas Riese, in
two articles, regards Dickinson as the master of
the absence présente: the significance of the present is revealed only when the "present" has turned
into the "past" (see footnotes 45 and 47). The
absence présente links Dickinson to the French
Symbolists. Martin Schulze, in his literary history, sees content and form as one in Dickinson's
poetry, a viewpoint that has increasingly won acceptance (see footnote 48). The last two publications of the decade, two books, are by Klaus
Lubbers and Hans Galinsky. Lubbers devotes his
book entirely to the reception of Emily Dickinson
in the English-speaking Western world (see footnote 49). In "reception" he includes tributes,
such as drama and music, concerned with Dickinson's
poetry or person. Galinsky, in the half of his
book treating Dickinson, uses a close-reading
method that is part a French explication de texte
and part a traditionally German linguistic approach
in order to interpret some central Dickinson poems,
in addition to tracing her reception in Germany,
particularly in the field of translation (see footnote 51).

It is, perhaps, indicative of the reputation
of Emily Dickinson in Germany during the sixties-
seventies that most of the criticism comes from
scholars such as Lubbers, Galinsky, and Hagenbüchle.
Not only is there no dissenting voice but there is
increasing emphasis on the high-quality technique
and language of Dickinson's poetry (such as in the
case of the mastery of absence présente), a high
tribute from the nation that elevated philology,
nowadays linguistics, to the rank of a science.
Out of the three publications from the seventies
surveyed here, the introductions of two full-length
books (one a collection of translations) came from
Klaus Lubbers and one major article from Roland

Hagenbüchle. In the introduction to the Gertrud
Liepe translations, Lubbers discusses Dickinson's
"problematical" relationship with both God and
nature, a relationship that became increasingly
"tragic" and "skeptical" toward the end of her
life (see footnote 56). Lubbers concludes that
Dickinson is "a genius, modern and timeless at the
same time." Gertrud Liepe, the translator, is the
third woman in Germany to publish a major collection of translated Dickinson poems. Roland
Hagenbüchle sees "precision and indeterminacy" as,
in reality, one in Dickinson: by deliberate use of
what may look like indeterminacy, she achieves
precision. This is Hagenbüchle's way of analyzing
Dickinson's handling of absence présente, the
topic treated by Oppens and Riese earlier.
Lubbers, in the last item of the seventies, a collection of literary essays, in his historically
oriented introduction pays particular tribute to
the importance of Dickinson. The two essays devoted to the poetess are both by Riese; they both
present a mainly linguistic explication de texte
of two poems. Stressed again is the elusive
absence présente as being the core of the Dickinson achievement that linguists label monist: form
is content, and content is form.

VI. Conclusion

The European critical responses to Emily Dickinson covered in this study can best be understood
as cultural-psychological responses of the countries involved. These critical sensibilities seem
to have been especially responsive to two qualities
of the poetess: her celebration of the individual
and her uniquely personal linguistic voice.

A. The Cultural-Psychological Response: "This was a Poet"

Many of the reasons for responses to artistic-
intellectual endeavors are to be found in the cultural-psychological make-up of a nation. The major
features of this make-up are especially discernible
within small nations. In considering Sweden and
its eastern neighbor Finland, one may find Emil
Staiger's "theory of loneliness" particularly appropriate.[1] The often considerable distances between individuals outside the cities and the harsh-
ness of the winter climate of these two countries
in particular were probably some of the first fac-
tors operating in forming the reserved personali-
ties of the inhabitants of those countries. Sec-

[1]Emil Staiger, Swiss esthetician and professor
of German literature, coined the term "the art of
loneliness" in his Grundbegriffe der Poetik [The
Basic Properties of Poetry]. It is Staiger's
theory that of the literary genres, poetry is
closely connected with both physical and spiritual
isolation: the "lonely" individual, or nation, is
more likely both to produce and "receive," i.e.,
appreciate, poetry. This theory was particularly
stressed by Staiger in a series of lectures on the
art of Goethe in the Fall of 1966 and Spring of
1967 attended by the present writer. For more
information on Staiger, see in particular chapter
II, footnote 100.

ond, the very physical "loneliness" provided the
ideal breeding-ground for the inner loneliness
that stems from too many opportunities for con-
templation. As Staiger argues, this kind of na-
tion--or individual--produces poetry. The Swedes,
even if one goes back only to the beginning of the
eighteenth century, have produced a number of
first-rate poets.[2] In Swedish-speaking Finland of
the same period, Johan Ludvig Runeberg and
Zacharias Topelius are poets whose reputations
have not been dimmed by time. In the twentieth
century, many major poets are found among the
Dickinson critics: Erik Blomberg, Johannes Edfelt,
Artur Lundkvist, Erik Lindegren, and Anders
Österling. While there are no Nobel laureates
among the Swedish Dickinson specialists, it is an
interesting fact that many are--or were--members
of The Eighteen:[3] Edfelt, Lundkvist, Lindegren,
and Österling among them.

In looking at the Swedish (and Finnish) Dickinson critics, one finds that two striking facts
are the wide range of professions involved and the
wide range of the media which published the criticism. It seems safe to assume that it is the general high standing of poetry in these countries

[2]Hedvig Charlotta Nordenflycht ("feminist"
poet 250 years before the term existed); Carl
Michael Bellman who sang about "the typical
Swedish figure of Movitz, the sentimental artist"
(Josua Mjöberg, Svensk Litteraturhistoria
[Swedish Literary History], Lund: C. W. K.
Gleerups Förlag, 1946, p. 76); Anna Maria Lenngren
--a Swedish Anne Bradstreet; Esaias Tegnér; Erik
Gustaf Geijer; Erik Johan Stagnelius; and Carl
Jonas Love Almquist (mainly prose), to mention
only some very few.

[3]The Swedish Academy, which awards the Nobel
Prizes, has eighteen members and is most often referred to as The Eighteen; see chapter II, footnote 1.

that makes educated people from all areas of life--
editors-in-chief of prestigious newspapers or
magazines, such as Anders Yngve Pers and Olov
Lagercrantz, to the dentist Ellen Löfmarck--devote
so much time to Dickinson. Significantly, not
only professors teaching American literature write
on Emily Dickinson but academicians from other
areas as well; in other words, the interest in poetry cuts through the nation as a whole. The out-
lets for scholarly publications in Scandinavia
often vary from those in large European nations,
such as France and Germany, and likewise the United
States. In a small nation, the few scholarly
journals existing cannot provide space for a large
number of highly qualified publishing scholars.
Thus in all of the Scandinavian countries, one
finds well-known names publishing mainly in the
"cultural pages" of daily newspapers, both in the
capitals and out in the country. If the critic is
considered well-known enough, he often signs his
material by initials only (Mats Molander, Emil
Liedgren, and others in this study).

Within the range of Swedish poets mentioned,
there were from the beginning many women:
Nordenflycht and Lenngren are two of the best
known. Being a woman was never a great handicap
in Scandinavia. For example, one can observe the
important position in society of Nordic women as
early as the Icelandic Sagas. Women have taken an
active part in literary criticism and a considerable number may be found among Swedish Dickinson
critics: Abenius, Lindqvist, Löfmarck, Ridderstad,
Nyberg, Bolin, Halldén, Strandberg, Lund, and,
above all, Lindberg-Seyersted. The important role
of women must certainly be taken into account in
explaining the Swedish-Finnish response to the
American poetess.

Another factor related to the cultural situation is one regarding translations. Exactly who
translated Dickinson in these countries? In
Sweden, with the one exception of Löfmarck, there
is a strict line between critics and translators,

a fact that holds true for literary criticism in general, not only for Dickinson criticism. Translators are often poets, but rarely critics. Translators such as Blomberg, Edfelt, and Lindegren (who dedicated two poems to Dickinson) are poets of all-European stature. Edfelt is and Lindegren was a member of The Eighteen. Perhaps a reason for this strict division--so different from the ways of the French and the Germans--is the passion for specialization and perfection so typical in all areas of life in Scandinavia: one does only what one does best.

The cultural aspects of Swedish-Finnish Dickinson criticism provide a microcosmic version of Swedish criticism. The important name is Lars von Haartman, a professor of Zoology. He is a first-rate poet in his own right, and it is as a poet-translator-artist, not as a critic, that he has dealt with Dickinson's poetry (see frontispiece). Of the few Swedish-Finnish critics, Hakalax is a woman. Typically, they all, including Haartman, published in general literary magazines or daily newspapers.

In Norway, the situation is comparable to that in Sweden proper and Swedish-speaking Finland. The two outstanding names are Hagerup and Skard. The first is one of the best known poets in Scandinavia, a woman; the second is one of the best known professors and specialists in the area of American literature that Europe has produced. Here, too, there is evidence of a wide range of professions and interests among the critics: Hagerup is not an "academic" person in the ordinary sense of the word. There is also a parallel between the poetess Hagerup in Norway and the poet Lindegren in Sweden: both dedicated poems to Emily Dickinson, a kind of tribute not found in the other countries surveyed.

Denmark, linguistically so close to Norway, nevertheless presents--has always presented--a very different cultural picture. In countries

where one has yet to hear of Swedish crystal,
silver, furniture, and food items, Finnish rya
rugs and glassware, or Norwegian knitwear, Danish
furniture and food are not only well-known but best
sellers. The economic, and thus decision-making,
backbone of Denmark has always been mercantile;
its upper-middle class, as well as its politicians,
was drawn from enterprising, money-making families.
The practical, no-nonsense outlook of the Dane has
no counterpart elsewhere in Scandinavia or in
Finland--and the "theory of loneliness" does not
apply to Denmark. Consequently, one would not
expect the Danish temperament to be drawn toward
the isolated sensibility of Emily Dickinson. This
is a crowded country; in this respect, as well as
in the others mentioned above, Denmark has its
counterpart in England, the birthplace of the modern novel. These two countries, with their eager-
ness to sell and their generally international
outlook, have always been culturally similar; this
similarity even covers aspects of the two languages
with particular regard to features of pronuncia-
tion, as has been noted long ago by linguists. It
should come as no surprise that extremely little
has been written on Dickinson in Denmark; most of
what has been written, though, is highly appreciative.

In discussing the cultural background of the
France-Dickinson relationship, one might comment
that conditions in general were especially suitable for her acceptance. Not only in literature
but in other art forms as well, women had been
recognized for centuries. Furthermore, the French
higher educational system, definitely elite, has
always catered to and encouraged the "probing"
curiosity of the Frenchman in general. Whatever
is difficult, one would naturally go for -- and
this is true not only about a Jacques Cousteau.
This passion for exploring anything truly challeng-
ing apparently found outlet in the unconventional
poetic expression of Emily Dickinson. Moreover,
the excellence of education in conjunction with
the classical heritage of rhetoric contributes to

171

the generally high level of literary criticism in
France. Some distinguished criticism is to be
found in equally distinguished scholarly journals
catering to the academic world. With the abun-
dance of such scholarly publications, one finds
little literary criticism appearing in magazines
and newspapers in general-- contrary to the case
in the Scandinavian countries. Among the French
Dickinson critics, one finds one member of Académie
française, André Maurois, and other scholars of
wide European renown.[4] Curiously, few women in
France have written criticism on Dickinson. One
of the few is Léonie Villard who is as much a
translator as a critic. Even among the translators, the important names are those of men, such
as Simon, Berger, and Zweig. Perhaps the most
striking feature of French Dickinson criticism is
the blend of critical commentary and translations
by the critic. It is tempting to suggest that because of the excellent qualifications of the
French critics and because of the rhetorical heritage of the Romance cultures, the French critic
creates a forum for his own writing of poetry, as
it were, within the boundaries of his critical
essay--a poète manqué. Rare is the French Dickinson critic, as chapter IV has revealed, who does
not try his hand at translation. Sometimes the
effort has been highly successful, sometimes not.

   The other continental country surveyed, Germany, shows both cultural similarities and dis-
similarities to its western neighbor. Here, too,
society is highly stratified and the Dickinson
critics, with the exception of some translators,
are well-established in their fields, generally
English literature. This is particularly true for
the sixties and seventies when the German Dickinson criticism comes from some of the best known

[4]Jean Catel, Régis Michaud, Léon Bocquet,
Charles Cestre, Cyrille Arnavon, Alain Bosquet,
Robert Goffin (a Belgian), Guy Jean Forgue, and
others.

critical names in Europe, such as Klaus Lubbers, Hans Galinsky, Roland Hagenbüchle, and Teut Andreas Riese. Like the Scandinavians, the German critics do not in general attempt translations as part of their stock-in-trade; Hans Hennecke is one of the few exceptions. The translators of Dickinson's poetry--for instance, Maria Mathi, Lola Gruenthal, and Gertrud Liepe--have mostly published full-length books, with or without a commentary. Interestingly, almost all German translators of Dickinson are women. Considering the size of the German-speaking area of Europe, comparatively little has been written 'in the area of poetry criticism in general and Dickinson criticism in particular. Galinsky explains this phenomenon by the traditional favoring of fiction and drama on the part of both German critics and the general public, particularly in the field of American literature.[5] The socio-political situation of the country during several of the decades crucial in Dickinson criticism should not be overlooked. Political and economic unrest during this time did not encourage literary criticism. One might add that Staiger's "theory of loneliness" certainly does not apply to Germany, second only to Belgium and the Netherlands in population density and geographically squeezed in between the political aspirations and idealogies of its surrounding neighbors.

To show how the critical responses of these European countries focused especially on the two qualities of Dickinson's poetry will be the remaining subject of this study.

[5] In his *Wegbereiter Moderner Amerikanischer Lyrik*, Hans Galinsky observes that Germans have traditionally shown less interest in American poetry than in American fiction and drama. He proves his point by citing statistics of, for instance, scholarly publications on and translations of American poetry. For more information, see the beginning of chapter V and, in particular, footnote 2.

B. The Celebration of the Individual:
   "The Soul Selects her own Society"

Dickinson critics in America have often concentrated on death and love as the two major
themes in Dickinson's poetry. In all of the European countries surveyed, the critics are conscious
of these themes but have mainly regarded them as a
backdrop for, or part of, a much larger one--the
celebration of the individual.

The "celebration of the individual" is regarded as a significant overall theme in all of
the nations surveyed. In Sweden and Finland, the
appreciation of the individual is a logical consequence of the before-mentioned geographical
isolation and, thus, is a response that has centuries behind it. When the soul has no other
company to select but its own, this individual
soul will take on added importance. It is, perhaps, this sense of the worth of the individual
that is the strongest common denominator between
Emily Dickinson and the Swedes in Sweden proper
and in Finland. A vast majority of Swedish critics, predictably, have saluted the value of the
individual as the most laudable feature of Dickinson's poetry. So Edfelt welcomes the "irony" and
"boldness" of Dickinson's personal treatment of
religion. Lagercrantz, significantly, compares
her to the Swedish poet Gustaf Fröding, the nation's foremost poetic champion for individual
freedom. Jaensson's viewpoint is exactly the same,
although his example is Stagnelius, the epitome of
the isolated artist. Österling sees Dickinson's
poetry as a product of loneliness, a viewpoint
close to that of Staiger. Fehrman finds another
self-professed "loner"-poet to be the perfect comparison: Edith Södergran. Christoffersson,
Molander, Löfmarck, Frykman, and Lund are but a
few of those Swedes finding physical and ensuing
spiritual loneliness "functional." Lindegren
praises Dickinson's "independent soul." In Finland, many of Lars von Haartman's preferences in
translated Dickinson poems indicate his own feel-

ing for the individual contra society; or, the
clown who, better than the king, understands the
miracle of spring (see frontispiece).

In Norway, the few Norwegians critics pay
tribute to the importance of the individual in
Dickinson's poetry. Skard commends her "terrifying honesty"--in Scandinavia, as perhaps also
elsewhere, often a euphemism for the triumph of
the individual over society. Karner Smidt sees
parallels to Kierkegaard with his emphasis on the
individual and the often paradoxical existence of
that individual. Hagerup does see Dickinson as
neurotic. The term "neurotic," one might add, is
often the label society puts on the self-assertive
individual.

The Danes, more practical in outlook, have
made less of Dickinson's assertion of the individual, despite the fact that a comparison to
Kierkegaard might be expected. Sørensen, the most
important Danish name in Dickinson criticism, does
pay tribute to the importance of the individual as
he sees it in Dickinson's poetry. He comments on
the tension between her "boring" provincial surroundings and the span and strength of a soul that
saw beyond those trivialities. Anders Österling
finds the "transatlantic uniqueness" of Dickinson
and other major American literary figures (Poe,
Hemingway, Whitman, among others) to be a quality
stemming from the personality of the "loner."
Österling's comments might sum up the general admiration on the part of the Scandinavians for the
individual who conquers society.

There were diversified political-psychologi-
cal circumstances that gave rise to French exis-
tentialism in the mid-twentieth century, among
which were the sense of the absurdity of World
War II and the losses of Indochina and Algeria.
Moreover, the favoring of l'art pour l'art, closely related to the celebration of the individual,
was already almost a French institution. The traditional regard for the woman as artist is also

part of the appreciation of the individual. The
link between Emily Dickinson and Kierkegaard would
probably be more obvious to a Frenchman than to a
Dane. The insistence on love, erotic or otherwise,
a major theme in Dickinson's poetry, gives rein-
forcement to the concept of the rights of the individual. The theme of love, mostly sexual, is
stressed in French Dickinson criticism; Feuillerat
is the first to point out the "nude" and "passionate" side of Dickinson's poetry. To call Dickinson "indiscreet" is high praise. The influential
Cestre particularly praises the open sensuality of
Dickinson and commends her for "forgetting the
prudence of the Puritan moral code." Arnavon and
Murciaux both hail her "nude" sensuality. Goffin,
more than anyone else, pays tribute to a consciously sexually oriented artist, a tribute supported
by Normand and Forgue. In none of the countries
covered has Dickinson's expression of the right to
sexual fulfillment--associated with the rights of
the individual--been emphasized to the same degree.

        The problem of the individual versus society
is particularly complicated with regard to Germany.
Before the late 1920's, when Dickinson criticism
emerged, the importance of a collective society
had been emphasized dating back to Bismarck.
Later, there followed the periods of the Kaiser,
the Weimar Republic, and World War II. It can be
assumed that just as the French, weary after the
war, had turned in the twenties toward the explora-
tion of the individual, the same craving for the
assertion of the individual must have existed
among Germans. Contrary to the socio-political
development in France, however, Germany moved from
the Weimar Republic into the Nazi regime. While
there is no indication that American literature as
such was viewed with suspicion during this period,
it seems safe to assume that any celebration of
the rights of the individual, let alone the right
for it to select its own society, would have been
met with disapproval. After World War II, the
awakening sense of every individual being responsible for his actions and of every such individual

road being a "lonely" one fostered a new curiosity
about literature concerned with the individual.
There was an interest in Eliot, Pound, Hemingway,
Poe—and Dickinson. Lüdeke, as one German critic,
significantly sees part of Dickinson's fascination
in the fact that she was a truly American phenomenon, i.e., part of a nation where the individual
regards itself as the maker and keeper of both
physical and spiritual property. Oppens, in somewhat nostalgic tones, points to the traditional
role of the dissenter in Anglo-Saxon literature
and considers this role one of the major attrac-
tions in Dickinson's poetry. In addition to the
generally renewed interest in the individual within Germany, possibly the fact that American occupy-
ing forces were close at hand after World War II
may have played a role in generating a specific
interest in American literature, poetry or otherwise. One of the best—and earliest—examples of
the attraction of the Germans to Dickinson's celebration of the individual is the inclusion of the
poem "Each Life Converges to some Centre" in a
magazine for psychology: every individual is unique
and has his own needs, according to the thesis of
the ensuing article. Schirmer, like his wife,
Schirmer-Imhoff, emphasizes Dickinson's rapport
with the Metaphysical poets—his way of praising
the individualistic quality of her poetry. When
Gruenthal speaks of Dickinson's "passion for realization" and Lubbers of her "poems of definition,"
they refer to the kind of trauma that the individual must face alone. Spitzer's repeated comparison of Dickinson and perhaps the most individualistic of all French poets, Charles Baudelaire, is
the ultimate tribute to the individualistic quality in Dickinson. Those critics, whether in Germany, France, or elsewhere, who see and admire
similarities between Dickinson on one hand and the
Symbolists on the other, praise the quality of
selecting the individual over society. It is significant that almost all of the German and French
Dickinson critics of the sixties and seventies
praise her as a master of <u>absence présente</u>, a much-
coveted term of the Symbolists.

177

C. Linguistic Technique and Style:
"Much Madness is divinest Sense"

Preoccupation with the individual may, by ex-
tension, imply preoccupation with individual style.
Indeed, other than the conscious celebration of
the individual on the part of the poetess, most
European critics regard Emily Dickinson's use of
language as the most impressive aspect of her poetry. This admiration for linguistic artistry is
not surprising in Scandinavia and Finland--coun-
tries traditionally fond of poetry--if one assumes
that interest in poetry implies interest in language as such. Significantly, the first in Sweden
to emphasize specifically Dickinson's use of language is a poet, Johannes Edfelt; Dickinson is
called an "innovator" far ahead of her time. When
Lagercrantz compares Dickinson to Fröding, he pays
tribute not only to individualistic values as mentioned before, but also to supreme linguistic artistry.[6] In Finland, Roos and Hakalax praise the
"paradoxes and metaphors" of Dickinson's poetry as
novel and three of five theses treat linguistic
aspects.

In Norway, Hagerup and Skard, the two major
names in Dickinson criticism, praise the l'art
pour l'art in Dickinson's poetry (here Hagerup
comes close to a French appreciation) and the
"surrealistic" quality of the poet's language

[6]Other Swedish critics who reason along the
same lines include, for instance, Vg. [signature],
who was the first in Sweden to compare Dickinson
to Heine--a compliment to mastery of form rather
than novel subject matter; Österling (again, Heine
is the point of reference); Lindquist; Fehrman;
Levander; and, above all, Brita Lindberg-Seyersted.
Lindberg-Seyersted devotes an article to Dickinson's punctuation alone and her full-length book
on the poet suggests that the linguistic aspects
of Dickinson's poetry are definitely superior to
the thematic ones.

178

(Skard). Sørensen, the one major name in Danish Dickinson criticism, totally concentrates on linguistic-stylistic aspects: his major point is that form is content, a viewpoint that anticipates later French and German criticism.

The French critics often stress the inseparability of the assertion of individual rights (often exemplified by sexual rights) and the uniquely individual linguistic technique and style of the poet expressing these individual rights. J. Normand remarks that discovery of total reality is carnal in quality: "this is how poets are born." The carnal inspiration is often inseparable from the very language itself, as in the cases of Dante, Donne, and Dickinson. Mallarmé said that one makes poetry not with ideas but with words, thereby summing up the credo of the French Symbolists. This is the viewpoint most often suggested by the French critics; in Cestre's words, "she [Dickinson] sacrifices the finished form to the suggestive form of the expression"--like the French Symbolists.7 Forgue comments that love is only the instrument that permits Dickinson to conquer the eternal light by use of "dissonances and surprises," another way of synthesizing eroticism-individualism and linguistic devices. Another comparison common among the French critics is between Dickinson and the Imagists; Cahen, Arnavon, and Bosquet are among those critics. For a nation that sees such ties between Dickinson on one hand and the Symbolists and Imagists on the other, Kierkegaard and Rilke seem automatically to come to mind, not only as great individualists in gen-

___

7Catel, Zweig, Goffin, Forgue, Maurois, and Simon mention Baudelaire, Mallarmé, and Verlaine; Maurois and Simon find Dickinson's themes conventional, an unusually pejorative word in a French context. Arnavon comments that "all linguistic conventions [underlining mine]" are violated in Dickinson's language--the highest praise.

179

eral but as champions of an independent style as well. The favorite stylistic term of the Symbolists, the <u>absence présente</u>, is perhaps the aspect of Dickinson's linguistic mastery that is more often praised than any other.

This <u>absence présente</u>, i.e., the concept that what either is in the past, or is about to be, is the only "reality" the human mind can grasp, is even more praised, if possible, by the German critics.[8] Traditionally inclined toward linguistic interpretations, the German critics have concentrated their attention on Dickinson's efforts to find verbal equivalents for her concept of time. Hagenbüchle treats death in Emily Dickinson's poetry from this particular angle: death is the point in time where the immediacy and value of life are made clear. The sex act, too—to mention the other major theme, love—is a perfect parallel to death; the value of it becomes clear only when it is about to slip into the past. A look at different connotations of the word "die" in, say, Shakespeare's time points up the parallel. In Germany, as in France, the overall linguistic comparison is to the Symbolists, Kierkegaard and Rilke, and to the Metaphysical poets. This characteristic is particularly true of the major German critical names, such as Oppens and Hagenbüchle. Riese and Oppens, as well as Schulze before them, present a linguistic monist viewpoint: Emily Dickinson's language, in all its aspects, is not only appropriate—it is synonymous with meaning. Hagenbüchle goes even further in arguing that what may seem vague and "difficult" in Dickinson's language is so only because that language alone will suffice to achieve precision—the ultimate tribute to linguistic artistry.

There is an interesting paradox involved in the European treatment of Emily Dickinson. One thinks

[8]This is particularly true of Hagenbüchle and Riese.

of present-day Americans as descendants of immigrants who left their mother countries to find a home more sympathetic to the individual and his needs. Yet the voice of this loner-artist is often treated by American critics attempting to use traditional frames of reference such as definition in terms of themes and the influence of certain biographical facts on the artistic product. On the other hand, European critics in general--where a more traditionally oriented outlook might have been expected--have tended to value Dickinson as the artist in opposition to a traditional background, a conventional society, and the conventions of her mother tongue--an existential success.

Bibliography

Abenius, Margit. "Emily Dickinson." Bonniers
    Litterära Magasin, 7 (1934), 18-23.

----------. Kontakter. Stockholm: Bonniers, 1944,
    pp. 93-104.

Abildgaard, Ove. "To dikte af Emily Dickinson:
    'Sejren' og 'Fangen'." Aktuelt, 10 (1960), 30.

A. E. [signature]. "Emily Dickinson." Der Westen,
    June 12, 1898, Sec. 3, p. 1, and June 19,
    1898, Sec. 3, p. 1.

[no title]. Afton-Bladet, September 28, 1951, p.
    4.

Anderson, Carl L. Poe in Northlight: The Scan-
    dinavian Response to His Life and Work.
    Durham: Duke University Press, 1973.

----------. The Swedish Acceptance of American
    Literature. Philadelphia: University of
    Pennsylvania Press, 1957.

Ansermoz-Dubois, Félix. Emily Dickinson: Choix de
    Poèmes. Genève: Éditions du Continent, 1945.

Arnavon, Cyrille. Histoire Littéraire des États-
    Unis. Paris: Librairie Hachette, 1953.

----------. "La Poésie Contemporaine (1887-1917)."
    Les Lettres américaines devant la Critique
    Française. Paris: Societé d'Édition "Les
    Belles Lettres," 1951, pp. 123-36.

Aschehougs Konversasjonsleksikon. 20 vols. Oslo:
    H. Aschehoug og Co., 1979, IV, 771.

Asselineau, Roger. "French Reactions to Heming-
    way's Works between the Two World Wars." The

Literary Reputation of Hemingway in Europe.
Ed. Roger Asselineau. New York: New York
University Press, 1965, pp. 39-72.

----------, ed. The Literary Reputation of
Hemingway in Europe. New York: New York
University Press, 1965.

Bab, Julius. Amerikas neuere Lyrik. Bad Nauheim:
[no publisher], 1953.

Blom, Dagny. "Sea, Sun, and Noon: A Study of
Three Symbols in Emily Dickinson's Poetry."
M.A. Thesis University of Oslo 1976.

Blomberg, Erik. "Emily Dickinson: Tre dikter."
Bonniers Litterära Magasin, 9 (1936), 597-98.

---------,---- and Johannes Edfelt. Dikter. Stockholm:
Wahlström och Widstrand, 1949.

Bocquet, Léon. "La Littérature Américaine."
Nouvelle Revue Critique, 15 (April 1931),
157-68.

Bolin, Greta. "Om sommaren sköna." Svenska
Dagbladet, August 10, 1967, p. 12.

Bonniers Lexikon. Eds. Uno Dalén et al. 15 vols.
Stockholm: AB Nordiska Uppslagsböcker, 1963,
III, 972.

Bosquet, Alain. Anthologie de la Poésie Américaine
des Origines à Nos Jours. Paris: Librairie
Stock, Delamain et Boutelleau, 1956.

Breitholtz, Lennart, ed. Litteraturens klassiker
i urval och översättning. 18 vols.
Stockholm: Almqvist och Wiksell, 1974,
XVIII, 104-10.

Brekke, Paal. Amerikansk lyrikk: Et utvalg i
norsk gjendiktning. Oslo: Aschehoug og Co.,
1957, pp. 26-32, 119-22.

Brigdman, Richard. "Emily Dickinson: A Winter
    Poet in a Spring Land." Moderna Språk, 56
    (1962), 1-8.

Brockhaus Enzyklopädie. 20 vols. Wiesbaden:
    F. A. Brockhaus, 1968, IV, 708.

Brown, John. Panorama De La Littérature Con-
    temporaine Aux États-Unis. 1954; rpt. Paris:
    Librairie Gallimard, 1971.

Brunel, Pierre. "Le Corbeau (à propos de la trans-
    position par Claudel d'un poème d'Emily
    Dickinson)." Revue des Lettres Modernes,
    134-36 (1966), 113-18.

Bruns, Friedrich. Die Amerikanische Dichtung der
    Gegenwart. Leipzig und Berlin: Verlag B. G.
    Teubner, 1930.

Cahen, Jacques-Fernand. La Littérature Américaine.
    Paris: Presses Universitaires de France,
    1950.

Cargill, Oscar. The Novels of Henry James. New
    York: Macmillan, 1961.

Carlson, Stig. "Ett amerikanskt diktaröde."
    Morgon-Tidningen, June 3, 1950, p. 4.

Catel, Jean. "Emily Dickinson: Essai d'analyse
    psychologique." Revue Anglo-Américaine, 2
    (June 1925), 394-405.

_____. "Emily Dickinson: L'oeuvre." Revue
    Anglo-Américaine, 3 (December 1925), 105-20.

_____. "Poésie moderne aux États-Unis I."
    Revue des Cours et Conférences, 34 (May 15,
    1933), 210-23.

_____. "Poésie moderne aux États-Unis II."
    Revue des Cours et Conférences, 34 (May 30,
    1933), 345-66.

----------. Quelques Poèmes de l'Amérique Moderne.
Paris: Collection Dauphine, 1945.

----------. "Sur Emily Dickinson: A Propos de
Deux Livres." Revue Anglo-Américaine, 13
(December 1935), 140-44.

Cestre, Charles. La Littérature Américaine.
Paris: Librairie Armand Colin, 1945.

----------. Les Poètes Américains. Paris:
Presses Universitaires de France, 1948.

Christoffersson, Birger. "Emily Dickinsons
hemlighet." Stockholms-Tidningen, January
17, 1955, p. 4.

----------. "Emily Dickinsons teknik." Morgon-
Tidningen, May 4, 1953, p. 3.

Combecher, Hans. Muse in Amerika: Vom eigen-
willigen Weg amerikanischer Dichtung: Interpretationen. Die Neueren Sprachen, Supplement I [no date], pp. 13-23.

Copeland, Marie Elsa. "Le Créateur et la création
dans la poésie de Jules Supervielle et
d'Emily Dickinson." Diss. University of
Paris 1964.

Dhejne, Hans. [no title]. Sydsvenska Dagbladet
Snällposten, December 14, 1949, [C.A.].

Dickinson, Emily. Bolts of Melody: New Poems of
Emily Dickinson. Eds. Mabel Loomis Todd and
Millicent Todd Bingham. New York: Harper
and Brothers, 1945.

"Dickinson (Emily)." Grand Larousse
encyclopédique. 10 vols. Paris: Librairie
Larousse, 1961, IV, 65.

Dickinson, Emily. Letters of Emily Dickinson. Ed.
Mabel Loomis Todd. Cleveland: World Publish-

ing Company, 1951.

_____. Letters of Emily Dickinson. 3 vols.
Ed. Thomas H. Johnson. Cambridge, Mass.:
Harvard University Press, 1958.

_____. The Poems of Emily Dickinson. 3 vols.
Ed. Thomas H. Johnson. Cambridge, Mass.:
Harvard University Press. 1955.

Dupont, Ernst and Peter M. Cummings. 24 American
Poets From Bryant to the Present. København:
G. E. C. Gads Forlag, 1966.

Edel, Leon. Henry James: The Middle Years.
Philadelphia: Lippincott, 1962.

Edfelt, Johannes. "Detta var en poet." Dagens
Nyheter, April 4, 1941, p. 5.

_____. "Emily Dickinson och dr. Holland."
Dagens Nyheter, October 25, 1951, p. 5.

_____. "Två dikter av Emily Dickinson."
Ord och Bild, [n. v.] (1944), p. 583.

_____, ed. Världens bästa lyrik i urval.
Stockholm: Natur och Kultur, 1961.

Ekman, Nils. "Jag dog för skönheten."
Beklädnadsfolket, 8 (1961), 15.

Emily Dickinson. Ed. Alain Bosquet. Paris:
P. Seghers, 1957.

"Emily Dickinson--amerikansk klassiker." Östgöta
Correspondenten, July 15, 1950, Regnbågen p.
2.

Emily Dickinson: Gedichte. Ed. and trans. Lola
Gruenthal. Berlin: Henssel, 1959.

Emily Dickinson: Gedichte. Trans. Gertrud Liepe.
Afterword Klaus Lubbers. Stuttgart:

Phillips Reclam Jun., 1970.

Emily Dickinson: Poèmes. Trans. and introd. Jean
Simon. Paris: Pierre Seghers, 1954.

Emily Dickinson: Twenty Poems: Vingt Poèmes. Introd. Paul Zweig. Trans. Claude Berger and
Paul Zweig. Paris: Minard, Lettres Modernes,
1963.

Der Engel in Grau: Aus dem Leben und Werk der
amerikanischen Dichterin Emily Dickinson.
Ed. and trans. Maria Mathi. Mannheim: Kessler,
1956.

Fehrman, Carl. "Emily Dickinson på svenska."
Samtid och Framtid, 5 (May 1950), 312-13.

Feuillerat, Albert. "La Vie Secrète d'Une
Puritaine: Emily Dickinson." Revue des Deux
Mondes, 40 (1927), 668-91.

Focus Uppslagsbok. 6 vols. Stockholm: Almqvist
och Wiksell Förlag AB, 1979, II, 611.

Ford, Thomas W. Heaven Beguiles the Tired: Death
in the Poetry of Emily Dickinson. University,
Alabama: University of Alabama Press, 1966.

Forgue, Guy Jean. Emily Dickinson: Poèmes.
Aubier: Aubier-Flammarion, 1970.

Frank, Josef. "Emily Dickinson." Prisma, 6
(April 1947), 21-23.

Frykman, Erik. "Emily Dickinson och språket."
Svenska Dagbladet, May 31, 1968, p. 5.

----------. "Sångens blixtnedslag." Göteborgs
Handels-och Sjöfartstidning, March 17, 1966,
p. 3.

Galinsky, Hans. Wegbereiter Moderner Amerikanischer Lyrik: Interpretations-und

Rezeptionsstudien zu Emily Dickinson und
William Carlos Williams. Heidelberg: Carl
Winter Universitätsverlag, 1968.

Goffin, Robert. "Emily Dickinson." Fil d'Ariane
Pour La Poésie. Paris: A. G. Nizet, 1964,
pp. 250-66.

Granichstaedten-Czerva, Elizabeth. "Bildersprache
bei Emily Dickinson." Diss. University of
Vienna 1940.

von Haartman, Lars. "Amerikanska dikter." Nya
Argus, 10-11 (1970), 168.

----------. "Dikter av Emily Dickinson." Nya
Argus, 7 (1968), 96.

----------. "Fyra dikter av Emily Dickinson."
Nya Argus, 19 (1961), 289.

----------. Letter to author. 6 September 1977.

----------. Letter to author. 7 September 1977.

----------. "There's a certain Slant of light."
Nya Argus, 19 (1968), 293.

Hagenbüchle, Roland. "Precision and Indeterminacy
in the Poetry of Emily Dickinson." ESQ, 20
(1974), 33-56.

Hagerup, Inger. "Emily Dickinson." Vinduet,
[n.v.] (1949), pp. 419-24.

----------. "Emily Dickinson." Vinduet, [n.v.]
(1974), pp. 43-46.

----------. "Emily Dickinson: Elleve dikt."
Vinduet, [n.v.] (1974), pp. 41-43.

----------. "Emily Dickinson: En kvinnelig
lyriker." Urd, 4 (January 23, 1943), 53-54.

——————. Personal interview. <u>Vinduet</u>, [n.v.]
(1974), pp. 28-40.

——————. "To dikt om döden." <u>Bonniers</u>
<u>Litterära Magasin</u>, 5 (1944), 399.

Hakalax, Vivi-Ann. "USA-lyriker erkänd efter sin
död: Arvet efter Emily Dickinson—1700
opublicerade dikter." <u>Hufvudstadsbladet</u>,
September 8, 1973, Lördagsextra, p. 3.

Halldén, Ruth. "Levande dikt ur en frusen kvinna."
<u>Dagens Nyheter</u>, August 14, 1972, p. 4.

Hennecke, Hans. "Emily Dickinson: Gedichte."
<u>Europäische Revue</u>, 8 (April 1937), 297-301.

——————. <u>Gedichte von Shakespeare bis Ezra</u>
<u>Pound</u>. Wiesbaden: Limes, 1955.

Iklé, Charlotte. "Sag Alles Wahr, Doch Sag Es
Schräg." <u>Du, Schweizerische Monatsschrift</u>
[Zürich], 21 (1961), 63-64.

<u>Internationale Zeitschrift für Individual-</u>
<u>psychologie</u>, 6 (September-October 1928), 386.

Jacoby, John. "L'esthétique de la sainteté:
Emily Dickinson." <u>Le Mysticisme dans la</u>
<u>Pensée Américaine</u>. Paris: Les Presses
Universitaires de France, 1931, pp. 241-76.

Jaensson, Knut. "En postum diktarbana." <u>Dagens</u>
<u>Nyheter</u>, March 20, 1950, p. 5.

J. C. [signature]. "Dickinson (Emily)." <u>La</u>
<u>Grande Encyclopédie</u>. 20 vols. Paris:
Librairie Larousse, 1973, VII, 3845.

K.-E.H. [signature]. "The Amherst nun." <u>Upsala</u>
<u>Nya Tidning</u>, April 25, 1950, p. 7.

Keller, Wolfgang and Bernard Fehr. <u>Die Englische</u>
<u>Literatur von der Renaissance bis zur</u>

Aufklärung. Wildpark-Potsdam: Akademische
Verlagsgesellschaft Athenaion M.B.H., 1928.

Kher, Inder Nath. The Landscape of Absence: Emily
Dickinson's Poetry. New Haven: Yale University Press, 1974.

Klett, Ada M. "Doom and Fortitude: A Study of
Poetic Metaphor in Annette von Droste-
Hülshoff (1797-1848) and Emily Dickinson
(1830-1886)." Monatshefte für Deutschen
Unterricht, 37 (1945), 37-54.

Kvam, Wayne E. Hemingway in Germany: The Fiction,
the Legend, and the Critics. Athens: Ohio
University Press, 1973.

Lagercrantz, Olov. "Om Emily Dickinson." Svenska
Dagbladet, June 13, 1950, p. 7.

----------. [no title]. Svenska Dagbladet, April
8, 1946, p. 8.

Landquist, John. "Främsta skaldinnan i USA."
Afton-Bladet, July 25, 1950, p. 4.

Las Vergnas, Raymond. "Lettres anglo-américaines."
Hommes et Mondes, 10 (June 1955), 450-52.

Le Breton, Maurice. Anthologie de La Poésie
Américaine Contemporaine. Paris: Éditions
Denoël, 1948.

----------. "L'Éternel Problème de la Traduction."
Études Anglaises, 9 (January-March 1956),
90-91.

----------. Rev. of Emily Dickinson's Poetry:
Stairway of Surprise by Charles R. Anderson.
Études Anglaises, 14 (July-September 1961),
279.

Levander, Hans. "Gärdsmygen från Amherst."
Afton-Tidningen, May 16, 1950, pp. 2-3.

Leyris, Pierre. "Poèmes et Lettres d'Emily Dickinson." Mesures, 5 (July 1939), 125-39.

Liedgren, Emil. "Ett enda glas av himlen." Västmanlands Läns Tidning, March 22, 1950, p. 5.

Lilla Uppslagsboken. 11 vols. Malmö: Förlagshuset Norden AB, 1965, II, 899.

Lindberg, Brita. "Emily Dickinson's Punctuation." Studia Neophilologica, 37 (1965), 327-59.

----------. "Further Notes on a Poem by Emily Dickinson." Notes and Queries, 213 (May 1968), 179-80.

----------. "The Theme of Death in Emily Dickinson's Poetry." Studia Neophilologica, 37 (1965), 327-59.

Lindberg-Seyersted, Brita. The Voice of the Poet: Aspects of Style in the Poetry of Emily Dickinson. Cambridge, Mass.: Harvard University Press, 1968.

Lindegren, Erik. "Den osynlige läsaren." Bonniers Litterära Magasin, 17 (1944), 903-05.

----------. "Två dikter för speldosa till Emily Dickinsons ära: Parafras och Gravskiss." Göteborgs Handels-och Sjöfartstidning, March 9, 1967, p. 3.

Lindqvist, Ebba. "Emily Dickinson efter många år." Ord och Bild, [n.v.] (1946), pp. 581-85.

----------. "Emily Dickinson presenteras." Göteborgs Handels-och Sjöfartstidning, April 13, 1950, p. 3.

Link, Franz. "Vier Gedichte Emily Dickinsons." Die Neueren Sprachen, 3 (1954), 406-13.

Lubbers, Klaus. Emily Dickinson: The Critical
Revolution. Ann Arbor: University of Michigan Press, 1968.

----------. "Einleitung." Die Amerikanische
Lyrik: Von der Kolonialzeit bis zur Gegenwart.
Ed. Klaus Lubbers. Düsseldorf: August Bagel
Verlag, 1974, pp. 11-20.

Lüdeke, Henry. Geschichte der Amerikanischen
Literatur. Bern: A. Francke Verlag, 1952.

Lund, Ann-Marie. "Skulle Emily ha gift sig med
pastorsadjunkten?" Dagens Nyheter, August
31, 1972, p. 4.

Lundkvist, Artur. Diktare och Avslöjare i
Amerikas Moderna Litteratur. Stockholm:
Kooperativa förbundets bokförlag, 1942.

Löfmarck, Ellen. "Den ensamma damen från Amherst."
Idun, 23 (June 1949), 8, 9, 18.

----------. Emily Dickinson. Stockholm: Bröderna
Lagerström, 1950.

----------. "Emily Dickinsons brev." Dagens
Nyheter, June 18, 1951, p. 2.

----------. "Emily Dickinson och offentligheten."
Dagens Nyheter, May 26, 1956, p. 4.

----------. "Emily, ensamheten och Gud." Dagens
Nyheter, January 8, 1960, p. 4.

----------. "Gåtan Emily Dickinson." Dagens
Nyheter, May 11, 1952, p. 4.

----------. "Resan till Amherst." Dagens Nyheter,
January 3, 1960, p. 4.

Matthiessen, F. O. American Renaissance. London
and New York: Oxford University Press, 1941.

Maurois, André. "Emily Dickinson: Poétesse et
     Recluse." Revue de Paris, 60 (November 1954),
     1-13.

----------. Robert et Elizabeth Browning:
     Portraits suivis de quelques autres. Paris:
     Bernard Grasset, 1955.

Meidinger-Geise, Inge. Rev. of Emily Dickinson:
     Gedichte by Lola Gruenthal. Welt und Wort,
     14 (1959), 349.

Meyers Enzyklopädisches Lexikon. 25 vols.
     Mannheim: Bibliographisches Institut, 1972,
     VI, 761.

Michaud, Régis. "Emily Dickinson." Dictionnaire
     biographique des auteurs. 2 vols. Paris:
     S.E.D.E. et V. Bompiani, 1956, I, 422-23.

----------. Panorama de la Littérature Américaine
     Contemporaine. Paris: Simon Kra, 1926.

Mjöberg, Josua. Svensk Litteraturhistoria. Lund:
     C.W.K. Gleerups Förlag, 1946, p. 76.

Molander, Mats. "Emily Dickinson." Dagens Nyheter,
     March 7, 1957, p. 10.

Monto, Marja. "Religious Metaphors and the Theme
     of Religiosity in the Poetry of Emily Dickin-
     son." M.A. Thesis University of Helsingfors
     1977.

Murciaux, Christian. "Emily Dickinson." Cahiers
     du Sud, 51 (April-May 1961), 276-89.

Møller, Niels. Verdens Litteraturen. København:
     Gyldendalske Boghandel Nordisk Forlag, 1929,
     p. 687.

Normand, J. "Emily Dickinson: une aventure
     poétique." Études Anglaises, 21 (1968),
     152-59.

Norstedts Uppslagsbok. Stockholm: P. A. Norstedt
och Söners Förlag, 1973, p. 265.

Nyberg, Ven. [no title]. Svenska Dagbladet, July
10, 1950, p. 5.

Oppens, Kurt. "Emily Dickinson: Überlieferung und
Prophetie." Merkur, 14 (January 1960), 17-40.

Papajewski, Helmut. "The Critical Reception of
Hemingway's Works in Germany since 1920."
The Literary Reputation of Hemingway in
Europe. Ed. Roger Asselineau. New York:
New York University Press, 1965, pp. 73-92.

[Pers, Anders Yngve]. "Färdigdiktat om Emily
Dickinson." Västmanlands Läns Tidning,
February 16, 1972, p. 12.

Pollitt, Josephine. "Emily beyond the Alps."
Saturday Review, 29 (April 6, 1946), 20.

----------. "In Lands I Never Saw." Guests in
Eden. Ed. Alma G. Watson. New York: Zeta
Chapter Phi Delta Gamma, 1946, pp. 34-37.

Quinn, Patrick. The French Face of Edgar Poe.
Carbondale: Southern Illinois University
Press, 1971.

Ridderstad, Stina. "En klassisk amerikansk
skaldinna." Östgöta Correspondenten, March
24, 1950, Regnbågen p. 2.

Riese, Teut Andreas. "Das Gestaltungsprinzip der
Konkretion in der neueren amerikanischen
Lyrik." Jahrbuch für Amerikastudien, 8.
Heidelberg: Carl Winter Universitätsverlag,
1963, 136-47.

----------. "Emily Dickinson: As imperceptibly
as Grief." Die Amerikanische Lyrik: Von der
Kolonialzeit bis zur Gegenwart. Ed. Klaus
Lubbers. Düsseldorf: August Bagel Verlag,
1974, pp. 157-62.

----------. "Emily Dickinson: Like Some Old fashioned Miracle." Die Amerikanische Lyrik: Von
der Kolonialzeit bis zur Gegenwart. Ed. Klaus
Lubbers. Düsseldorf: August Bagel Verlag,
1974, pp. 147-56.

----------. "Emily Dickinson und der Sprachgeist
amerikanischer Lyrik." Die Neueren Sprachen,
12 (1963), 145-59.

Roos, Alarik. "Poesin som struktur." Hufvudstadsbladet, October 3, 1949, p. 9.

----------. "Överraskningarnas skaldinna."
Hufvudstadsbladet, December 9, 1967, p. 7.

Rovit, Earl. "The Shape of American Poetry."
Jahrbuch für Amerikastudien, 6. Heidelberg:
Carl Winter Universitätsverlag, 1961, 122-33.

Schirmer, Walter F. Kurze Geschichte der
Englischen Literatur: Von den Anfängen bis
zur Gegenwart. Halle-Saale: Max Niemeyer
Verlag, 1945.

Schirmer-Imhoff, Ruth. Rev. of Letters of Emily
Dickinson. Ed. Mabel Loomis Todd. Anglia,
71 (1953), 365-66.

Schulze, Martin. Wege der amerikanischen Literatur: Eine geschichtliche Darstellung.
Frankfurt am Main: Ullstein, 1968.

Skabo, Lise and J. Meyer-Myklestad. A History of
English and American Literature for Schools.
Oslo: Gyldendal Norsk Förlag, 1968.

Skard, Sigmund. American Studies in Europe: Their
History and Present Organization. 2 vols.
Philadelphia: University of Pennsylvania
Press, 1958, II, 439-41.

----------. "Emily Dickinson: Det analytiske
auga." Verdens litteraturhistorie. 12 vols.

Oslo: Cappelens Forlag A. S., 1973, IV, 384-92.

_____. "Emily Dickinson - det analytiske Øje." Verdens litteraturhistorie. 12 vols. Ed. Per Nykrog. København: Politikens Forlag, 1973, IX, 387-95.

_____. "Hemingway in Norway." The Literary Reputation of Hemingway in Europe. Ed. Roger Asselineau. New York: New York University Press, 1965, pp. 127-50.

_____. Under nye Stjerner: Amerikansk lyrikk gjennom 300 år. Oslo: Gyldendal Norsk Forlag, 1969, pp. 20-23, 92-107.

Smidt, Aagot Karner. "Emily Dickinson." Vinduet, [n.v.] (1961), pp. 220-23.

Spitzer, Leo. "Baudelaire, Les Fleurs du Mal: LXXVII--Spleen." Interpretationen zur Geschichte der französischen Lyrik. Heidelberg: Selbstverlag des Romanischen Seminars der Universität Heidelberg, 1961, pp. 170-79.

_____. "Baudelaire's 'Spleen'." Romanische Literaturstudien. Tübingen: Max Niemeyer Verlag, 1959, pp. 286-93.

Stewart, Katherine Kenyon. "French Criticism of Four American Poets: Poe, Whitman, Dickinson, Robinson." M.A. Thesis University of Kansas 1938.

[no title]. Stockholms-Tidningen, September 19, 1949, p. 5.

[no title]. Stockholms-Tidningen, April 11, 1958, p. 13.

Strandberg, Kerstin. "Motroten." Dagens Nyheter, August 28, 1972, p. 5.

197

Svensk Uppslagsbok. 32 vols. Malmö: Förlagshuset
    Norden A. B., 1955, VII, 354-55.

Sørensen, Paul. "Emily Dickinson." Moderne Ame-
    rikansk Lyrik: Fra Whitman til Sandburg.
    København: Borgens Billigbøger, 1965, pp.
    152-73.

----------. "Emily Dickinsons Digte." Berlingske
    Aftenavis, December 15, 1950, Kronik pp. 6, 8.

Thomas, J. Wesley. Amerikanische Dichter und die
    Deutsche Literatur. Duderstadt: Volksbücherei
    Verlag Goslar, 1950.

Verdenslitteraturen: Hvem skrev hvad før 1914.
    5th ed. Ed. Henning B. Fonsmark. København:
    Politiken, Politikens Litteraturhåndbøger,
    1969, pp. 157-58.

Vg. [signature]. [no title]. Morgon-Tidningen,
    October 24, 1949, p. 5.

Villard, Léonie, La Poésie Américaine: Trois
    Siècles de Poésie Lyrique et de Poèmes
    Narratifs. Paris: Bordas Frères, Les
    Éditions Françaises Nouvelles, 1945.

Vordtriede, Werner. "Die Puritanische Droste."
    Neue Deutsche Hefte, 6 (December 1959), 857-
    59.

The World Book Encyclopedia. 20 vols. Chicago:
    Field Enterprises Educational Corporation,
    1969, IV, 156.

Åhnebrink, Lars. "Hemingway in Sweden." The
    Literary Reputation of Hemingway in Europe.
    Ed. Roger Asselineau. New York: New York
    University Press, 1965, pp. 151-76.

Österling, Anders. "Emily Dickinson på svenska."
    Stockholms-Tidningen, March 27, 1950, p. 4.

Österling, Anders. [no title]. Stockholms-
    Tidningen, October 31, 1949, p. 5.

INDEX OF NAMES

Kjørsvik, Liv Reidun, 70n
Klett, Ada M., 137-38, 161-
   62
Kvam, Wayne E., 1n

L

Lagercrantz, Olov, 12-13,
   26-27, 56, 169, 174, 178
Landquist, John [J. L.],
   28, 56, 109, 127
Las Vergnas, Raymond, 104
Lawrence, D. H., 117, 131n
Le Breton, Maurice, 99-100,
   105-07, 110, 125-27
Lenngren, Anna Maria, 168n
Levander, Hans, 25, 56, 178n
Lewis, Sinclair, 2n, 6
Leyda, Jay, 66, 121, 160
Leyris, Pierre, 95, 98n,
   123n, 125
Liedgren, Emil [Lgn.],
   21, 56, 169
Liepe, Gertrud, 156, 165,
   173
Lind, Jenny, 132-33
Lindberg, Brita (Lindberg-
   Seyersted, Brita), 37-38,
   39n, 40-42, 51, 57, 154n,
   169, 178n
Lindegren, Erik, 12, 39, 55,
   58, 168, 170, 174
Lindqvist, Ebba, 13n, 14,
   23-24, 55-56, 169, 178n
Lindvall, Lars, 46
Link, Franz, 141-42, 162
Longfellow, Henry Wadsworth,
   88, 150, 158
Lowell, Amy, 153
Lowell, James Russell, 107
Lowell, Robert, 118, 121,
   155

Lubbers, Klaus, 131n, 153-54,
   156-58, 159n, 160n, 163-65,
   173, 177
Lund, Ann-Marie, 44-45, 48, 58,
   98n, 169, 174
Lundkvist, Artur, 10-11, 55-56,
   168
Lüdeke, Henry, 139-40, 157n,
   162, 177
Löfmarck, Ellen, 14-16, 18-19,
   21-25, 27-30, 32-34, 47-48,
   52n, 55-58, 78, 169, 174

M

Mallarmé, Stéphane, 1n, 104,
   112-13, 158, 179
Martinson, Harry, 31
Marvell, Andrew, 118
Mathi, Maria, 143-44, 162-63,
   173
Matthiessen, F. O., 1
Maurois, André, 103-05, 109,
   126, 172, 179n
Meidinger-Geise, Inge, 145-
   47
Melville, Herman, 36, 66, 102n,
   118, 147, 156
Meyer-Myklestad, J., 67n, 79,
   81
Michaud, Régis, 87-88, 101,
   119, 123-24, 172n
Milton, John, 42
Mjöberg, Josua, 168n
Molander, Mats [Mm.], 32, 34n,
   57, 169, 174
Monet, Claude, 149, 163
Monto, Marja, 53n, 54n
Moody, William Vaughn, 96,
   101n, 125
Moore, Marianne, 118, 121
Murciaux, Christian, 108-10,
   127, 176

Møller, Niels, 73

N

Newton, Sir Isaac, 106, 126
Nietzsche, Friedrich, 147–
48, 163
Nordenflycht, Hedvig Char-
lotta, 168n, 169
Normand, J., 116–17, 118n,
128, 176, 179
Nyberg, Ven [V. N.], 27, 169
Nykrog, Per, 77n

O

O'Neill, Eugene, 156
Oppens, Kurt, 147–48, 151n,
159, 163, 165, 177, 180

P

Papajewski, Helmut, 133
Partanen, Raili, 53n
Pasternak, Boris, 116
Patterson, Rebecca, 29–31,
57, 66, 109
Pers, Anders Yngve, 42n, 169
Poe, Edgar Allan, 1, 2n, 9,
75, 90n, 103, 109, 118–20,
147, 149–50, 153n, 158,
175, 177
Pollitt, Josephine, 94, 121–
22, 124
Pound, Ezra, 52n, 76, 78,
118, 131, 142, 153, 158,
177

Q

Quinn, Patrick F., 1n

R

Reitmayer, Sabine, 154n
Ridderstad, Stina [F. Ch.],
20n, 21–22, 56, 169
Riese, Teut Andreas, 150–52,
158–59, 163–65, 173, 180
Rilke, Rainer Maria, 147–48,
158, 163, 179–80
Robinson, E. A., 73n, 90
Roos, Alarik, 49–51, 58, 178
Rovit, Earl, 149, 164
Runeberg, Johan Ludvig, 168

S

Sappho, 31, 62, 135, 161
Schirmer, Walter F., 136, 161,
177
Schirmer-Imhoff, Ruth, 141,
162, 177
Schulze, Martin, 152–53, 164,
180
Scott, Kate Anthon, 30–31, 109
Shakespeare, William, 14, 42,
95, 103, 142, 180
Shelley, Percy Bysshe, 103, 109
Sihto, Pirkko, 53n
Simon, Jean, 102–07, 126, 172,
179n
Sjöberg, Birger, 5, 12, 25
Skabo, Lise, 67n, 79, 81
Skard, Sigmund, 2, 7n, 64–68,
70, 77, 79, 170, 175, 178–
79
Smidt, Aagot Karner, 66–67, 79,
175
Spinoza, 106, 126

Ö

Österling, Anders, 6, 16–17,
22–23, 56, 168, 174–75, 178n

INDEX OF DICKINSON POEMS

211

About the Author

Ann Lilliedahl has spent long periods of her life in various European countries. In addition to her Ph.D. in English, she has done graduate work in German and French having studied at Uppsala University, Sweden, Würzburg University, Germany, Zürich University, Switzerland, and Sorbonne University, Paris, France. She is Associate Professor of English at Texas Southern University, Houston, Texas.